Training Tenor Voices

Training Tenor Voices

Richard Miller

Schirmer Books

An Imprint of Macmillan Publishing Company
New York

Maxwell Macmillan Canada
Toronto

Maxwell Macmillan International
New York   Oxford   Singapore   Sydney

Schirmer Books
An Imprint of Macmillan Publishing Company
866 Third Avenue
New York, NY 10022

Maxwell Macmillan Canada, Inc.
1200 Eglinton Avenue East, Suite 200
Don Mills, Ontario M3C 3N1

Macmillan Publishing Company is part of the Maxwell
Communication Group of Companies

Library of Congress Catalog Card Number: 91-25936

Printed in the United States of America

printing number
1 2 3 4 5 6 7 8 9 10

Library of Congress Cataloging-in-Publication Data

Miller, Richard, 1926–
    Training tenor voices / Richard Miller.
        p.   cm.
    Includes bibliographical references (p.   ) and index.
    ISBN 0-02-871397-4
    1. Singing—Instruction and study.   2. Tenors (Singers) — Training
of.   I. Title.
    MT820.M6   1992
    782.8'7143 — dc20   91-25936
                                                                 CIP
                                                                 MN

The paper used in this publication meets the minimum requirements of
American National Standard for Information Sciences — Permanence of
Paper for Printed Library Materials. ANSI Z39.48 –1984.   ∞™

TO THE MEMORY OF JUSSI BJOERLING

Contents

Preface

It is well known that there are fewer tenors than other male vocal categories. The baritone is the norm of the male voice. Tenor and bass voices are
aberrations from that norm, and are therefore highly prized in the vocal
performance world. Although all singers perform best when they use their
vocal instruments efficiently, the tenor requires an even higher level of
precise function than do other singers, a fact often overlooked or misunderstood by teachers accustomed to the typical medium-low-voiced male,
the baritone. (There are special problems in dealing with the bass voice,
but they are not germane here.)

One frequently hears that there is today a crisis in tenors. Of course
there is. There always has been. Such a crisis is due to the physical deter-
minants of vocal categories, with a lower percentage of male vocal instruments being congenitally constructed to serve as potential professional
tenor singers, and to the lack of adequate training for this category of male
voice. Many of the psychological problems assumed to beset some tenors
can be explained by their having been taught little about the specific technical handling of their *Fach* (category). The technically secure tenor is as
stable as any singer, and stereotyped tenor jokes are symptomatic of the
lack of understanding about the performance demands and technical requirements of tenor voices.

Singing teachers often comment on the difficulty of teaching tenors.
Seldom does a teacher confess to problems in teaching sopranos, mezzos,
baritones, or even basses, yet many teachers admit that teaching the tenor
voice remains a mystery. As a result, the typical professional tenor is a
singer who, like Tamino, has undergone a series of trials; he succeeds
against a number of predetermined unexplained odds, including vocal
pedagogies that remain silent about the special nature of the tenor singing
instrument. The tenor is often successful because, all theater folklore to the
contrary, he usually possesses a solid native intelligence and an indestruc-
tible psyche. In no other category must the singer face a similar volume of
myths with regard to everything from brains to sexual prowess. Tenors
have these commodities in equal proportion to other male vocal categories.

The tenor voice has traditionally been associated with heroic sensual-
ity, partly because of the combination of high fundamental frequencies
(pitches) and virile energy demanded by the literature assigned to this
voice. Perhaps the tenor vocal instrument most nearly exhibits, in the
cultivated singing voice, the ancient Greek ideal—unification of beauty and
strength—that forms the traditional aesthetic of the Western world.

Performance tasks of the tenor exceed those of other vocal categories.

Most opera roles for tenor voice call for more vocal stamina and greater dramatic subtlety than do the villain/character roles generally assigned to lower-voiced males. The frequent charge that tenors are lesser actors than baritones fails to take into account the inherent difference in the degrees of difficulty between acting tasks: singing a physically and emotionally strenuous love duet with a large dramatic soprano is far more difficult than is the seducing of an attractive soubrette, a duty that usually falls to the baritone.

A study to determine the percentage of tenors, compared to other vocal categories, who have become conductors, stage directors, company managers, impresarios, and professors of singing, might reveal unexpected results. The tenor personality (and there is such a thing) tends to display a combination of energy and ability to take risks and accept challenges. Why not? Singing tenor *is* a challenge. It requires guts and intelligence. It also demands the best technical foundation a singer can get. This book (whose author is willing to accept risks and challenges, it would appear) aims to be helpful in supplying some practical information.

Acknowledgments

This book is dedicated to the memory of Jussi Bjoerling, perhaps the greatest tenor technician of the century, whose vocal proficiency, artistry, and professional objectivity serve as inspiration and goal to all tenors. I am indebted also to a number of other famed tenors, past and present, for the technical discipline they display, which permits high levels of skillful vocalism to serve as enviable models for many of us who also sing tenor, or who teach tenors.

On a more practical level, I wish to express my thanks to Robert Axelrod and Garrett Schure, Schirmer Books/Macmillan, for the patience and care exercised in the difficult tasks associated with the production of this book. Thanks also go to Dave Schilling of Tecnicom Corporation for his generous assistance in reproducing some anatomical illustrations, to Tom Abelson, M.D., for reading parts of the manuscript, and to George Ullman (Boosey & Hawkes), Richard Walters and Nancy Ubick (Hal Leonard Publishing), Fred Koch (International Music) and especially to Iris Torres (G. Schirmer) for their assistance in locating sources of musical examples or for granting permission for their use.

Much of the information in this work was gathered during Oberlin College faculty development grants, and other research projects carried out at the Otto B. Schoepfle Vocal Arts Laboratory, Oberlin College Conservatory, which was established through the generosity of the Kulas Foundation, Cleveland, Ohio, and the *Elyria Chronicle Telegram*, Elyria, Ohio.

I must express my warmest appreciation to a young tenor, Juan Carlos Franco, research assistant at the Otto B. Schoepfle Vocal Arts Laboratory, for his invaluable help in the final preparation of this book.

Finally, Mary, my wife, deserves my eternal gratitude for the help she cheerfully extends to all the enterprises in which I am involved, including this study. She could certainly write an authoritative book on the behavior of tenors!

Training Tenor Voices

Chapter 1

Classification of Tenor Voices

To speak of "the tenor voice" as though all tenors belonged to an identical category is to ignore the great variety that exists within the tenor tribe. In large part, it is the location of registration events, the *passaggi*, at certain points in the ascending scale, that determines several subdivisions within the overall tenor vocal category. For that reason, this work on training tenor voices begins with the subjects of vocal registration and vocal classification.

REGISTER EVENTS

The phenomenon of vocal registers has long interested teachers of singing and voice researchers. Manuel Garcia's definition is still useful:

> By the word register we mean a series of succeeding sounds of equal quality on a scale from low to high, produced by the application of the same mechanical principle, the nature of which differs basically from another series of succeeding sounds of equal quality produced by another mechanical principle. (Manuel Garcia, 1840, *Mémoire sur la Voix Humaine*, p. viii.)

There is a wide range of viewpoints regarding the incidence of registers in the singing voice. There are teachers who deny the existence of registers, and there are others who claim there are as many as seven. Part of the confusion arises from the skill with which the professional singer learns to negotiate the scale evenly so as to eliminate any suggestion of register transitions. The aim of all good vocal technique is to develop an even scale without register demarcations, unless register contrasts are desired for reasons of style or expression. Reports of perceptual studies on vocal registers frequently are confusing because the trained singer does not display the sudden register shifts that the researcher finds in amateur or student-level singing unless the singer expressly wishes them. (We should be skeptical of scientific studies that purport to use "professional opera singers"; they often include student-level performers.)

Even though the pivotal register points of each tenor category are relatively predictable, the structure of an individual larynx and vocal tract, and the proprioceptive responses of the singer, offer a number of variations within basic registration practices.

As with all male voices, the lower singing range of the tenor closely parallels that of his speaking voice. If a male places the palm of his hand on his sternum (breastbone) when he is speaking, he feels a vibratory rumble. As he inflects his voice upward into a higher speaking range, the vibratory sensation diminishes. The same phenomenon occurs when he sings a mounting scale. Notes below the upper limits of comfortable speech inflection make up the register of the male voice known traditionally as *voce di petto* (chest voice). The term "chest" describes the location of vibratory sensation in lower range.

In 1962 van den Berg commented on the generally accepted viewpoint that vibrations originating below the larynx are assumed to be gradually damped on their way down toward the alveoli and that subglottic air has no resonant properties that can influence the larynx ("Some Physical Aspects of Voice Production," *Research Potentials in Voice Physiology*, pp. 63–64). Van den Berg went on to express his own surprise in discovering that in measuring subglottic pressure variations in a subject, he found resonant properties that he could only ascribe to the subglottic system.

William Vennard (*Singing: The Mechanism and the Technique*, p. 86) states that

> every time a compression wave is created above the glottis, the pressure below the glottis is decreased; that is, a rarefaction wave is formed; and *vice versa*. The pattern which goes up also goes down. The fact that it is in reverse makes no difference, the frequencies are all the same.

It is clear that the lungs, which are filled with air, cannot be resonators, but it is probable that some form of resonance from the trachea (and to a lesser degree, the bronchi) and the laryngeal response to it, contributes to the vibratory sensation in the male lower range ("chest" voice). Whatever the eventual determination of the actual contribution of vibrating subglottic air to vocalized sound, it is clear that the control of subglottic pressure is a major factor in both breath management and vocal registration. When the singer uses "chest" register, the chest *feels* like a resonator.

Research indicates that the cricothyroid muscles show increased activity as pitch rises. The vocal folds (also termed vocal bands and, currently with less frequency, vocal cords) elongate and the mass of the vocal fold diminishes. This stretching and thinning process increases with ascending pitch.

At certain points in the scale of each singer, changes in vocal timbre become perceptible (particularly in the untrained voice). Such changes come about because the laryngeal muscles do not remain in a static posture throughout the mounting scale. In an ascending scale, certain dynamic, as opposed to static, muscle activity occurs at pivotal register points described as "breaks," "lifts," or *passaggi*. There are corresponding changes in the resonator system above the larynx (and probably below). These events, together with laryngeal responses, determine the register phenomena of the singing voice.

Because it is psychologically not a good idea to speak of "breaks" in a voice, and because the term "lift" has connotations that are not restricted to vocal registration, the term *passaggio* (passage), whose plural is *passaggi*, is useful. The musician is accustomed to using Italian as the technical language of music, and by now the term *passaggio* is part of the international vocabulary of vocal pedagogy.

When a speaker arrives at the first register demarcation point (registration pivotal point), he must begin to use the "calling" voice in order to produce pitches that lie above the customary speech range. He can do this by increasing breath energy (airflow rate and subglottic pressure) and by raising the dynamic level (increasing decibels). He can continue to "yell" pitches that lie roughly a musically-notated perfect fourth above the first register demarcation point. This first pivotal point is the *primo passaggio* of international vocal terminology. A second pivotal point, approximately a fourth above the *primo passaggio*, is the *secondo passaggio*, beyond which a speaker cannot call without his voice "breaking" or without experiencing discomfort in the larynx.

The trained singer, however, can produce pitches above the *secondo passaggio* either by resorting to falsetto (the imitative sound of the female voice by the male) or by learning to sing *voce piena in testa* (full voice in head), the accepted public performance practice of the international school. The area between the two pivotal points (*primo passaggio* and *secondo passaggio*) is known as the *zona di passaggio* (passage zone). Whereas in the speaking voice a male must shout when using this range, the singer learns to avoid the "call" of the voice through the use of registration principles described later.

The *zona di passaggio* must be skillfully negotiated if there is to be no "break" when the "head" register becomes predominant. Dynamic balancing among the laryngeal muscles and the resonator tract enhances desirable gradual registration equalization and results in a registration timbre historically termed *voce mista, voix mixte* (mixed voice), or *voce media* (middle voice). Herman Klein, noted critic on vocal practices in the nineteenth century, wrote in *The Bel Canto* (1923):

> With the aid of this *voix mixte*, the union of the "chest" and "medium," of "medium" and "head" tones, proceeding either up or down the scale, the voice can be brought into line throughout the whole compass. (p. 22–23)

The mechanical action among thyroarytenoid and cricothyroid muscles that produces the equalized scale is described by otolaryngologist/singer Donald Proctor (1980, "Breath, the Power Source for the Voice," *The NATS Bulletin*), as follows:

> There is some controversy over the nature of the so-called "break" in the voice. One can raise the pitch of the voice considerably by increasing vocal cord tension alone, and without lengthening the vocal folds. In my opinion,

the elimination of this troublesome vocal problem, this "break," requires that one learn how gradually to bring in the vocal fold lengthening process at a lower pitch than it ordinarily would come into play. Thus, as a scale is sung, there is a smooth transition from increasing vocal fold tension to vocal fold lengthening. (p. 30)

The dynamic muscle balance within the laryngeal mechanism that brings about this equalization is illustrated in Figure 1.1.

The vocal folds have layers of tissue that include a body (the vocalis muscle), a transition, and a cover (composed of the vocal ligament and the mucosa). The structure of a single vocal fold is illustrated in the schema of Figure 1.2. When the cricothyroid muscles contract and the vocalis muscles are less active, the vocal fold lengthens and its tissues tighten (see Figure 1.3); with these changes, the fundamental frequency (what the listener perceives as pitch) rises.

By contrast, if the vocalis muscles contract and the cricothyroid mus-

FIGURE 1.1.   Schematic design of graduated registration activity in the tenor voice. The *passaggi* indicate a lyric tenor.

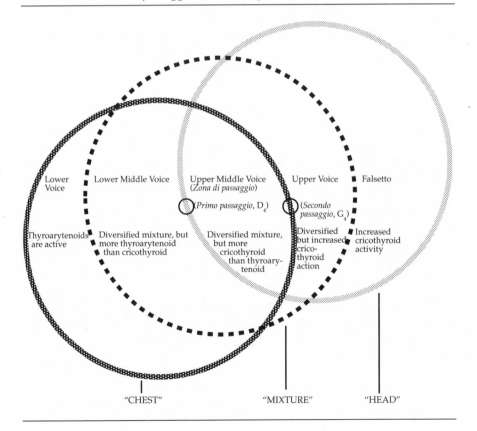

FIGURE 1.2. Schematic cross-section of vocal fold cover, transition, and body.

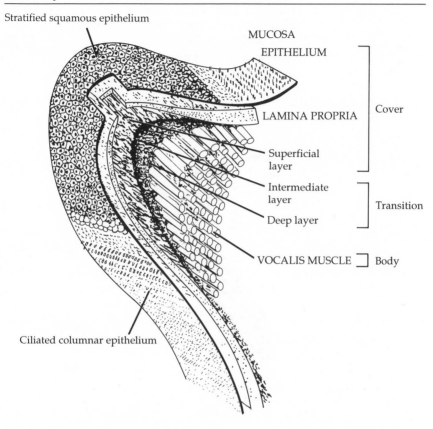

Stratified squamous epithelium

MUCOSA

EPITHELIUM ⎤

LAMINA PROPRIA

Superficial layer ⎦ Cover

Intermediate layer ⎤

Deep layer ⎦ Transition

VOCALIS MUSCLE ⎤ Body

Ciliated columnar epithelium

Vocal Fold Physiology, edited by Kenneth N. Stevens and Minoru Hirano. Tokyo University Press, 1981. By permission.

cles become less active, the vocal fold length decreases, and there is a corresponding decrease in the stiffness of the cover. Even when the vocal fold length decreases, it is still possible for some degree of stiffness to remain in the body of the folds (Titze, 1981, *The NATS Bulletin*). It is the degree of activity between cover, vocalis muscle, and the cricothyroids that contributes to smoothness or abruptness of registration events in the singing voice. The varying degrees of stiffness in tissues of the vocal folds, then, result from coordinating the groups of internal laryngeal muscles, all subconsciously controlled by the singer's concept of vocal timbre and through his acoustic responses (by what he hears). This is not a static condition but a dynamic coordination, constantly changing for the requirements of pitch and power—what Titze calls *differential* control as opposed to *uniform* control of muscle groups. In short, there must be no postural fixing of the registration process, no "hooking in," no muscular setting.

FIGURE 1.3. The dashed line and upper arrow show the kind of sliding motion postulated to occur between cover and body. The possibility of a vertical force on the cover is indicated by the arrow at the bottom.

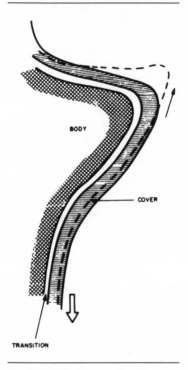

BODY

COVER

TRANSITION

Vocal Fold Physiology, edited by Kenneth N. Stevens and Minoru Hirano. Tokyo University Press, 1981. By permission.

The results of such differential registration controls have been schematically illustrated in Figure 1.1. Figure 1.4 further depicts graduated registration in the lyric tenor voice. The *tenore lirico* generally has his *passaggi* at D_4 and G_4 (the *zona di passaggio* lies between them). (Frequency designations [pitches] are indicated by the U.S.A. Standards Association system shown in Figure 1.5) The same schema can be used to illustrate registration events in other tenor categories by adjusting the *passaggi* points accordingly.

The cricothyroids are mostly responsible for lengthening the vocal folds. They change the relationship between the cricoid cartilage and

FIGURE 1.4. A schematic design of lyric tenor registration events.

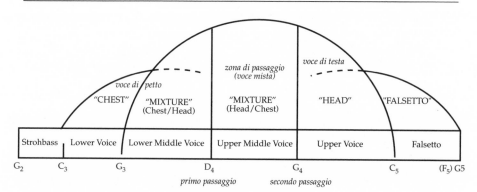

| Strohbass | Lower Voice | Lower Middle Voice | Upper Middle Voice | Upper Voice | Falsetto |

G₂ C₃ G₃ D₄ G₄ C₅ (F₅) G5

primo passaggio   *secondo passaggio*

thyroid cartilage, thus contributing to the alteration of pitch. Figure 1.6 shows various positions of the vocal folds and the arytenoid cartilages in abduction (opening of the glottis) and in adduction (closing of the glottis). Figure 1.6(f) illustrates the function of the cricothyroid muscles as they increase the length of the vocal folds; Figure 1.6(g) represents the shortening of the vocal folds in response to the thyroarytenoid muscles.

Increased thyroarytenoid activity is associated with "chest" voice, while increased cricothyroid activity is associated with "head" voice. The vocal fold tissues respond in complex ways within both actions, and the two forms of muscle function do not occur completely independent of each other. The vocal folds elongate and thin for the singing of high pitches and they shorten and thicken for low pitches. The cricothyroid muscles largely determine vocal fold length. A dimension of vocal fold activity of importance to vocal registration concerns the changing relationship between the vocalis muscles and the vocal ligaments. Van den Berg succinctly described

FIGURE 1.5. U.S.A. Standards Association pitch designations. The less-currently-used Helmholtz designations are indicated beneath the U.S.A. Standards Association symbols.

| C_1 | C_2 | C_3 | C_4 | C_5 | C_6 | C_7 |

U.S.A. Standards Association

| C_1 | C | c | c^1 | c^2 | c^3 | c^4 |

Helmholtz

Permission by *The NATS Journal*.

FIGURE 1.6.   A series of diagrams to show different positions of the vocal folds and the arytenoid cartilages.

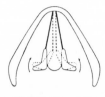

(a) Position of rest in quiet respiration. The intermembranous part of the rima glottidis is triangular and the intercartilaginous part is rectangular in shape.

(b) Forced inspiration. Both parts of the rima glottidis are triangular in shape.

(c) Abduction of the vocal folds. The arrows indicate the lines of pull of the posterior cricoarytenoid muscles. The abducted vocal folds and the abducted, retracted and laterally rotated arytenoid cartilages are shown in dotted outline. The entire rima glottidis is triangular.

(d) Adduction of the vocal folds. The arrows indicate the lines of pull of the lateral cricoarytenoid muscles. The adducted vocal folds and the medially rotated arytenoid cartilages are shown in dotted outlines.

(e) Closure of the rima glottidis. The arrows indicate the line of pull of the transverse arytenoid muscle. Both the vocal folds and the arytenoid cartilages are adducted, but there is no rotation of the latter.

(f) Tension of the vocal folds, produced by the action of the cricothyroid muscles which tilt the anterior part of the cricoid cartilage upwards and so carry the arytenoid cartilages backwards.

(g) Relaxation of the vocal folds, produced by the action of the thyroarytenoid muscles, which draw the arytenoid cartilages forwards.

Gray's Anatomy, 37th British edition, edited by Robert Warwick and Peter Williams. Edinburgh: Churchill Livingstone, 1980. By permission.

this activity in 1968 at the symposium "Sound Production in Man," New York Academy of Sciences:

> When the subject sings an ascending or a descending scale with no appreciable transition in sound quality, he needs to change gradually from one type of adjustment to the other. That means that the active tensions in the vocalis muscles and the passive tensions in the vocal ligaments, together with the adduction of the glottis and the value of the flow of air, need to balance smoothly and gradually. (p. 131)

Vocal registration is not entirely laryngeal and supraglottic, but is in part dependent upon subglottic pressure and airflow factors.

The location of the subtle changes in dynamic muscle balance necessary to the equalized scale depends, in part, on vocal category. Several subcategories exist within the generic tenor voice.

THE CATEGORIES OF TENOR VOICE

Tenorino

The clearest exposition of the differences in tenor categories may be made by looking first at the lightest of tenor voices, the *tenorino*. *Tenorino* timbre is produced by the male with a high speaking voice who sometimes is dubbed a "true tenor" by persons who know little about the professional voice. "Irish tenor" is another designation for this vocal type, although that description does not take into account the number of Irish men who skill-fully sing tenor but who do not fit the *tenorino* category. The *tenorino* is generally a person of slight build with thin neck structure and a relatively prominent Adam's apple (vocal prominence). It is also possible, but un-usual, to find a very light tenor instrument lodged in the physically robust individual. The register pivotal points for the *tenorino* occur at higher pitches than for other tenors—sometimes at E_4 for the *primo passaggio*, with A_4 as the *secondo passaggio*.

The *tenorino* may avoid legitimate "head voice" timbre (which results from firmer muscle balance in upper range) because he can sing through his *zona di passaggio* without registration modification until arriving at his *secondo passaggio*, beyond which he unites his light instrument with fal-setto. He (or his teacher) may mistakenly assume that he is using legiti-mate "head" voice.

Because of the size limitation of the *tenorino* instrument, there may be good reason for the singer to incorporate the easy falsetto production into the upper range in a manner not appropriate to tenor voices of professional size. Many amateur and choir tenors fall into the *tenorino* category and may fail to find the *voce di testa* register. Professional performance opportunities for this category of tenor are generally limited, although in the heyday of radio several sweet-voiced *tenorini* were much admired.

Tenore leggiero (tenore di grazia)

The *tenore leggiero* (light tenor) shares some of the characteristics of the *tenorino*, but his voice is of sufficient size and quality to be considered a viable professional instrument. His *passaggi* points are most likely at $E_4^\flat$ and $A_4^\flat$, and he does not always sing easily in the lower (*voce di petto*) range. He is also called (less frequently than formerly) *tenore di grazia* because composers often assigned to him florid writing rich in coloratura passages and vocal embellishments. His timbre is generally characterized by sweetness (*morbidezza*), and he must possess considerable control over musical dynamics. In the nonoperatic literature he may excel at early Ba-roque music or the works of Bach. If his voice is of fair size and if the performance hall is not too large, he may be useful in lighter Mozart, Donizetti, Bellini, and Rossini roles. Vocal grace and flexibility are required of him more than of any other type of tenor. Some typical roles are Ottavio (*Don Giovanni*), Conte (*Il Barbiere di Siviglia*), Nemorino (*L'Elisir d'amore*), Ernesto (*Don Pasquale*), Fenton (*Falstaff*) and light roles of the French repertoire. He must be able to compete with his colleagues in ensembles and be heard over an orchestra, as must any professional singer.

Spieltenor

A special category of tenor is found in the German theater. The *Spieltenor* instrument is similar to the *leggiero* but usually has a wider capability, being able to take on somewhat heavier roles than the *leggiero* can manage. At times the *Spieltenor* is assigned lesser roles of the lyric tenor repertory. His voice is most suited to roles such as Arturo (*Lucia di Lammermoor*), Jaquino (*Fidelio*), Pedrillo (*Die Entführung aus dem Serail*), David (*Die Meistersinger von Nürnberg*), Schouisky (*Boris Godunov*), Fenton (*Die Lustigen Weiber von Windsor*), Vaček (*Bartered Bride*), Cassio (*Otello*), and Beppe (*I Pagliacci*).

His *passaggi* may be those of the *leggiero* if he is on the light side of the category, or more like the *lirico* (see below) if his voice is somewhat heavier. Above all, he must be a fine singing actor. He may have to content himself with the better character roles, not solely because of his vocal instrument but because of his slight physical build. The *Spieltenor* is often vocally and physically the male counterpart of the *soubrette*.

Tenore buffo

The *tenore buffo* is yet another category of light tenor voice. In the non-Germanic theater the *buffo* repertory encompasses roles sung by the *Charaktertenor* and some of those sung by the *Spieltenor*. However, a distinct timbre usually identifies his vocal type. The *tenore buffo* may well be able to execute much of the literature sung by his *leggiero* and *Spieltenor* colleagues, but his vocal timbre often suffers from a *Knödel* (the sound of a dumpling in the throat), that is, an *ingolata* (throaty) quality. This distinctive sound is largely the result of techniques that assume the throat is best opened for singing by excessive spreading of the pharyngeal wall. A number of light tenor voices exhibit this throaty quality, partly in response to the desire for a larger sound.

The *buffo* tenor is usually small in stature. He is neither physically nor psychologically convincing when playing romantic roles unless they are also humorous in nature. He is often the henchman, the minor villain, the obsequious servant, the buffoon, the foolish cuckold, or the lower-class friend of the hero. Typical roles are Monostatos (*Die Zauberflöte*), Dancairo and Remendado (*Carmen*), Guillot (*Manon*), Cajus and Bardolfo (*Falstaff*), Goro (*Madama Butterfly*), Spoletta (*Tosca*), Gherardo (*Gianni Schicchi*), and Valzacchi (*Der Rosenkavalier*).

Operetta tenor

The tenor who sings operetta in the German and French theaters is not generally expected to sing opera roles. His is a specialized career in acting and singing. He must have a voice of romantic character but with some of the timbre of the music-hall singer. He must cut a handsome figure (often more theatrical than believable), with stage-movement facility that matches the superficiality of the musical style. Generally, his voice is not adequate for the sturdier lyric operatic roles, although for operetta it must be of good size and quality and be technically secure. Many roles of "classic" operetta make demands equal to those of the lyric tenor operatic repertory, but the theatrical setting allows for less intensity both vocally and dramatically. Typical repertory is the genre of J. Strauss, Lortzing, Millöcker, Offenbach (excepting *Les Contes d'Hoffmann*), and the works of Lehar, Friml, and Romberg.

The *musical-comedy tenor* is a near relative of the operetta tenor. Although generally trained as a "classical" singer, the tenor performing musical comedy must modify his singing in matters of diction and timbre to fit the entertainment circumstances under which he performs. (However, romantic leads in musical comedy often are given to the baritone, not the tenor.)

Tenore lirico

The *tenore lirico* (lyric tenor) is the "ideal" tenor for much of the standard operatic literature. His *passaggi* points typically occur at D_4 and G_4. His timbre must be warm, romantic, exciting, and vital. He must have the ability to sustain a high *tessitura* and to negotiate the upper range with beauty and vigor. His *Fach*, although varying with the precise weight of the individual lyric tenor instrument, typically encompasses such roles as Tamino (*Die Zauberflöte*), Ferrando (*Così fan tutte*), Ottavio (*Don Giovanni*), Alfredo (*La Traviata*), Duca (*Rigoletto*), Rodolfo (*La Bohème*), Pinkerton (*Madama Butterfly*), Rinuccio (*Gianni Schicchi*), Des Grieux (*Manon*), Sänger (*Der Rosenkavalier*)), Flamand (*Capriccio*), and Tom Rakewell (*The Rake's Progress*).

Much of the oratorio literature, especially that of Handel, lies conveniently for the *tenore lirico*, as does a major part of the *Lied* and *mélodie* genres. The lyric tenor is a highly useful vocal category because of the wide range of appropriate literature.

Tenore lirico spinto

There is a fine line to be drawn between the *tenore lirico* and the *tenore un po' spinto* (a little *spinto*—from *spingere*, "to thrust"). Differences depend on vocal weight and the response of a particular tenor to specific roles. For example, the *La Bohème* Rodolfo lies fabulously well for some lyric tenors, while for others it is overly dramatic. The same is true of Pinkerton, Duca, and Des Grieux. These roles, however, are ideal for the *lirico spinto* who is able to retain lyricism in his singing. His *passaggi* points tend to fall at $C_4^\sharp$ and $F_4^\sharp$.

The *lirico spinto* has all the advantages of the *tenore lirico,* but in addition he has the power and vocal impact to deliver the dramatic aspects of the Verdian and *verismo* repertories. He combines sheer vocal beauty with dramatic thrust. The union of lyricism and power makes this type of tenor the most prized of all male vocal categories. Native timbre and weight of the individual operatic tenor voice determine which roles should be assigned. These often include Don José (*Carmen*), Faust (the Gounod *Faust*), Hoffmann (*Les Contes d'Hoffmann*), Manrico (*Il Trovatore*), Riccardo (*Un Ballo in Maschera*), Carlo (*Don Carlo*), Cavaradossi (*Tosca*), Turiddu (*Cavalleria Rusticana*), Walther (*Die Meistersinger von Nürnberg*), Lohengrin (*Lohengrin*), and Herman (*Pique Dame*). In some cases, the true *spinto,* especially as he matures, may cautiously attempt a few of the *robusto* roles, although this has proved unwise for many singers. The weight of these roles often demands a heavier production than is suited to the *spinto* instrument.

Tenore robusto, tenore drammatico

The *tenore robusto* is the heaviest of all non-Wagnerian tenors. His *passaggi* are typically C_4 and F_4 and parallel those of some lyric baritones. He is frequently a large person of compact build, and although he may be tall, he usually is short necked and barrel chested. He must have the stamina and the power to portray Radames (*Aïda*), Canio (*I Pagliacci*), Otello (*Otello*), Calaf (*Turandot*), Tito (*La Clemenza di Tito*), Florestan (*Fidelio*), Samson (*Samson et Dalila*), and Bacchus (*Ariadne auf Naxos*). He may also sing some *spinto* roles.

Heldentenor

The *Heldentenor* is a specialist. He is chiefly a Wagner singer. His fate is Tannhäuser (*Tannhäuser*), Siegmund (*Die Walküre*), Tristan (*Tristan und Isolde*), Siegfried (*Götterdämmerung*), and Parsifal (*Parsifal*). Given current expectations of vocal timbre and weight in the Wagnerian voice, his life is not easy. (How closely these expectations accord with Wagner's own intent could make an interesting debate.) The *Heldentenor* in many German-language houses is also expected to sing the Italian *robusto* literature. Generally, his success at the Italian literature is not remarkable.

Some "heroic" tenors emerge, in vocal maturity, from the baritone *Fach*. These singers tend to continue registration practices more appropriate to the baritone than to the tenor category. With some frequency, the *passaggi* of this *Fach* are identical to those of the *tenore robusto* (C_4–F_4), but some current *Heldentenors* have *passaggi* points as low as those of the *Heldenbariton* (heroic baritone)—near $B^\flat_3$ and $E^\flat_4$—and they manage upper pitches of the voice by pushing up "chest voice" function far beyond healthful practice.

WHEN TO SING WHAT

Determining the *Fach* of a singer is not the primary concern for the teacher. Of much greater importance is the freeing of the instrument from the tensions of malfunction and from preconceived ideas that so often contribute to incorrect vocal production. Only then is it possible to determine the eventual vocal category. The developmental continuum must be kept in mind when one determines what any singer should currently sing.

The young, potentially professional tenor, approximately age twenty-four to twenty-seven, should study none of the *spinto* or *robusto* roles, regardless of his eventual vocal category. That literature must wait until he is in his early thirties. When Caruso died, Gigli (who performed exceedingly well into his mid-sixties) at age thirty-one wisely refused to take on the heavier roles he later sang at age forty.

COMMENT ON THE COUNTERTENOR

The countertenor is not here given extensive consideration because, generally, he is not a tenor. Most often he is a baritone who has made the decision to develop the falsetto register as his chief performance vehicle. No pejorative judgment is made regarding that decision. Countertenor timbre appeals to the current taste for expanded vocal sound. Countertenoring is a viable way to perform certain literatures. The countertenor is, in fact, here to stay. Alfred Deller's success in applying a cultivated falsetto to literature previously neglected by the modern male solo singer opened new performance doors. The exploding recording business has created numerous opportunities for the male falsettist.

There are several ways to sing countertenor. Falsetto register plays a more prominent role in some of these techniques than in others. Without doubt, however, falsetto is crucial to all of them. It is naive to assume that there exists a rare type of vocal instrument known as "the countertenor" based on specific laryngeal construction. Almost any musical male singer can learn to use falsetto in a skillful manner; that is, he can learn to sing countertenor if he so chooses.

Falsetto production does not require the same degree of laryngeal muscle activity as that needed for the fully registered male voice. For that reason, falsetto is easy to accomplish. It permits agile movement in the execution of rapid passages and embellishments, and allows for an easy control of dynamics. Falsetto does not involve the fullest functions of the completely coordinated male singing voice, and in no way is it identical with *voce piena in testa* (full head voice).

Although falsetto production provides an easier existence, in most regards the countertenor still must deal with problems common to all male voices. He has an additional concern: because of his frequent reliance on a register in which vocal fold occlusion is either incomplete or produced through less-efficient muscle balance, the countertenor often evidences a high rate of breath emission. It is possible through the use of enhanced technical means to mitigate some of the built-in functional disadvantages that come from singing falsetto. The *appoggio* system of breath coordination (see Chapter 2) becomes even more essential in countertenoring than in more efficient forms of singing. Agreement between vibrator (larynx) and resonator (vocal tract) must be as precise as possible in order to minimize the inefficient function that results when falsetto serves as the main performance register. Sections of this book that deal with establishing good breath management and accurate vowel tracking are especially important for the male falsettist. (Assertions that the countertenor in some way recovers the sound of the castrato are, of course, not to be taken seriously.)

Chapter **2**

Breathing for Singing

Techniques of breath coordination should be uniform among singers, yet registration and vowel modification requirements of specific vocal categories determine changing levels of airflow and subglottic pressure during the mounting scale. Learning to manage airflow and subglottic pressure demands a subtle coordination of aerodynamic-myoelastic factors (airflow and muscle responses) that is the foundation of cultivated singing.

THE PHYSICAL BASIS

A number of techniques for breath management (breath coordination) for singing are based on false assumptions regarding physiological function. Action is sometimes attempted among muscle groups that cannot perform the breathing tasks imaginatively assigned them. For example, many procedures for "controlling the diaphragm" have little or nothing to do with diaphragmatic function during the breath cycle, especially during phonation. Even the location of the diaphragm is often misunderstood; actions of the abdominal and intercostal muscles during expiration frequently are mistakenly attributed to the diaphragm itself.

The diaphragm cannot be discerned by surface observation, nor does it register proprioceptively. It is the large muscle that separates the respiratory system from the digestive system. Its position in the torso is much higher than many singers imagine; the central tendon of the diaphragm is attached to the pericardium, in which the heart is housed. The diaphragm cannot be "fixated" by pulling inward on the abdominal wall. Nor does it go down for high pitches and up for low ones. Most investigators confirm that the diaphragm makes little or no direct contribution to the "support" of the voice because during expiration the diaphragm (as registered by EMG [electromyography]) mostly remains electrically silent. Movements of the diaphragm are, in part, dependent upon actions of the neighboring musculature. The intercostals and the muscles of the torso help determine diaphragmatic position. The teacher who instructs a singer to control the diaphragm can only be referring to neighboring muscle controls. Some of the activity of the muscles of the abdominal wall and the torso *can* be externally observed.

As the thorax expands in inhalation, the diaphragm descends; as the abdominal wall moves inward, the diaphragm ascends. The position of the

15

diaphragm is also dependent on intrapleural and intra-abdominal pressures. During exhalation, the elastic recoil of the lungs tends to pull the diaphragm and the abdominal viscera upward during the normal breath cycle. In the *appoggio* technique of breath management for singing, the weight and activity of the abdominal viscera (the guts) delay the upward movement of the diaphragm. The diaphragm and the musculature of the torso and the abdomen are here indicated in a series of figures. (See Figures 2.1–2.6.)

During the singing of extended phrases, the sternum remains elevated and the rib cage expanded; the abdominal muscles must retain their antagonistic relationships (counteracting, not tensing), remaining as long as is comfortable near the inspiratory position. In this manner, the expiratory gesture of the breath cycle is delayed, and the tendency toward inward contraction of the abdominal wall is retarded. Such postural attitudes may best be described as "maintaining the noble position."

A normal, quiet inhalatory-expiratory breath cycle, without phonation, requires about four seconds, approximately one second for inhalation and three for exhalation. In speech, this cycle may be extended for additional seconds before breath renewal takes place. Singing, however, often requires phrases of much longer duration than does speaking, and at higher frequency (pitch) levels. Therefore, the normal breath cycle appropriate for speaking is not sufficient for the needs of the singing voice.

Unfortunately, some vocal techniques unwittingly induce a more rapid

FIGURE 2.1. The abdominal surface of the diaphragm.

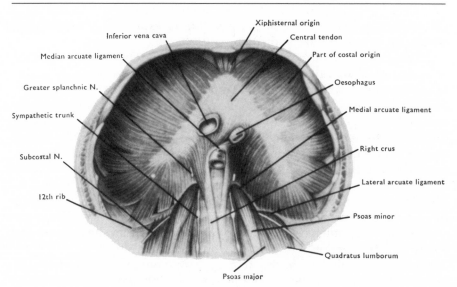

Cunningham's Manual of Practical Anatomy, Vol. 2, 14th ed., edited by G. J. Romanes. Oxford University Press, 1977. By permission.

FIGURE 2.2. Muscles of quiet inspiration.

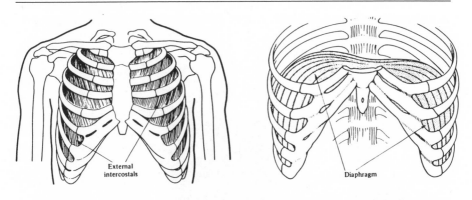

External intercostals

Diaphragm

Thomas J. Hixon, "Respiratory Function in Speech," in *Normal Aspects of Speech, Hearing, and Language*, Minifie, Hixon, and Williams, eds., p. 84. Reprinted by permission of Prentice Hall, Inc., Englewood Cliffs, New Jersey, 1973.

diaphragmatic ascent and inward abdominal movement than is necessary, because the assumption is made that breathing for singing must correspond to the "natural" breath processes of speaking. Breathing for singing, although based upon principles of natural function, does *not* exactly mirror the events of the normal breath cycle found in speech. Breath coordination for singing is an acquired skill dictated by breath-management requirements that are not needed for everyday life.

In the breath cycle, the external intercostal muscles and the intercartilaginous intercostal muscles raise the ribs; the interosseus internal intercostals depress the ribs. Their actions are partly dependent upon the positioning of the entire torso, the sternum in particular (see Figures 2.3, 2.4, 2.6, and 2.7).

Because the sternum occupies a central position in the topography of the thorax, it is a major player in determining the extent of costal expansion and diaphragmatic excursion. It does so not through activation but through its postural function. The first two ribs are attached to the upper portion of the sternum (the manubrium) (see Figure 2.3). If the sternum remains relatively high and is maintained in that posture throughout the breath cycle, the muscle relationships exhibited by the thorax are different from those that occur when the sternum is lowered.

In inhalation, the diaphragm moves downward and presses the abdominal viscera forward, causing the abdominal wall to expand slightly outward. When this action is complete, the abdominal viscera form a steady base so that muscle fibers of the central tendon of the diaphragm can assist in elevating the ribs. In this way the lower ribs are elevated and expanded, and lung volume increases.

The smallest air cells in the lung are called alveoli. Decrease in the intrathoracic pressure, which occurs with inhalation, permits air to flow

FIGURE 2.3. Muscles of the neck, thorax, and abdomen.

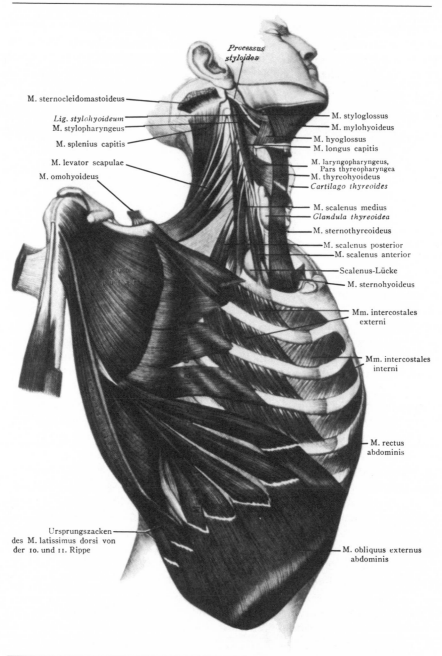

Toldt, C./Hochstetter, F.: *Anatomischer Atlas*, 27th ed., 1979. Edited by Krmpotic Nemanic. Urban & Schwarzenberg, Munich. Reprinted by permission.

FIGURE 2.4. Muscles of the thorax and abdomen.

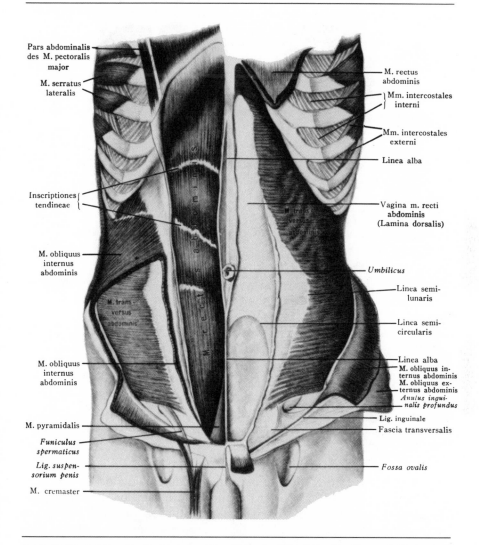

Pars abdominalis
des M. pectoralis
major

M. serratus
lateralis

M. rectus
abdominis

Mm. intercostales
interni

Mm. intercostales
externi

Linea alba

Inscriptiones
tendineae

Vagina m. recti
abdominis
(Lamina dorsalis)

M. obliquus
internus
abdominis

Umbilicus

Linea semi-
lunaris

Linea semi-
circularis

Linea alba

M. obliquus
internus
abdominis

M. obliquus in-
ternus abdominis
M. obliquus ex-
ternus abdominis
*Anulus ingui-
nalis profundus*

M. pyramidalis

Lig. inguinale

Fascia transversalis

*Funiculus
spermaticus*

*Lig. suspen-
sorium penis*

Fossa ovalis

M. cremaster

M. trans-
versus
abdominis

Toldt, C./Hochstetter, F.: *Anatomischer Atlas*, 27th ed., 1979. Edited by Krmpotic Nemanic. Urban & Schwarzenberg, Munich. Reprinted by permission.

into the alveoli because the total gas pressure in the lung is at that moment lower than the atmospheric pressure. Air does not have to be pulled into the lungs; like water, air seeks the lowest pressure level. Therefore, no need exists to develop breath techniques based on conscious or noisy efforts to fill the lungs with breath. Breath is not pulled into the lungs; it simply arrives there.

Muscles of the upper torso are of importance in maintaining good posture for freedom in breath management for singing. In the aforemen-

FIGURE 2.5. Muscles of the abdomen.

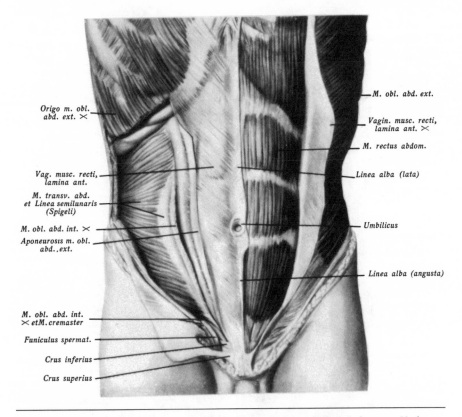

Origo m. obl. abd. ext. ×

Vag. musc. recti, lamina ant.

M. transv. abd. et Linea semilunaris (Spigeli)

M. obl. abd. int. ×

Aponeurosis m. obl. abd..ext.

M. obl. abd. int. × etM. cremaster

Funiculus spermat.

Crus inferius

Crus superius

M. obl. abd. ext.

Vagin. musc. recti, lamina ant. ×

M. rectus abdom.

Linea alba (lata)

Umbilicus

Linea alba (angusta)

Topographische Anatomie (1935), ed. by Wilhelm Lubosch. Munich: J. F. Lehmanns Verlag (Springer-Verlag). By permission.

tioned "noble" posture, muscles of the neck and torso permit the organs of breathing (lungs and diaphragm) to function maximally. The axial body (head, neck, and torso) must be well aligned; there should be no elevation or lowering of the chin; a relatively high sternal position is essential to such alignment.

The broad flat muscles of the abdomen protect the viscera and exert pressure on them, thereby helping to determine the position of the internal organs. The abdominal muscles respond to activity of the muscles of respiration and of those chest muscles that assist in maintaining good posture. The flexor abdominal muscles keep the muscles of the thorax in antagonism to the spinal muscles. The large flat abdominal muscles cross each other, lending support to this area of the torso, which is devoid of bony structure (see Figure 2.7).

A deeply located abdominal muscle is the transverse abdominis, which runs horizontally from the internal surface of the rib cage and

FIGURE 2.6. Origins and attachments of the muscles of the thorax and abdomen.

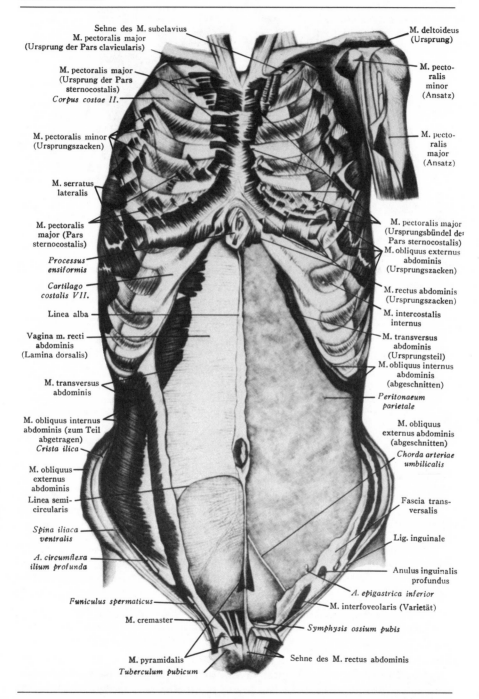

Toldt, C./Hochstetter, F.: *Anatomischer Atlas*, 27th ed., 1979. Edited by Krmpotic Nemanic. Urban & Schwarzenberg, Munich. Reprinted by permission.

FIGURE 2.7.   Muscles of the thorax and abdomen.

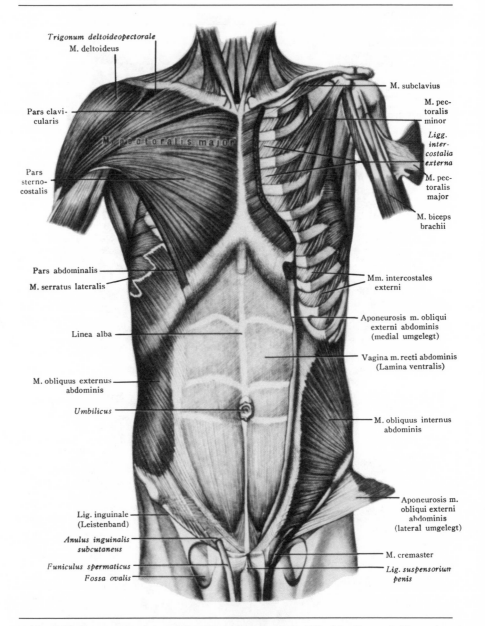

Toldt, C./Hochstetter, F.: *Anatomischer Atlas*, 27th ed., 1979. Edited by Krmpotic Nemanic. Urban & Schwarzenberg, Munich. Reprinted by permission.

crosses the torso (as its name implies) (see Figure 2.8). Its fibers lie at an angle to the fibers of two outer layers of fan-shaped muscles that arise from the external surfaces of the lower eight ribs and radiate downward

FIGURE 2.8. Muscles of the thorax and abdomen.

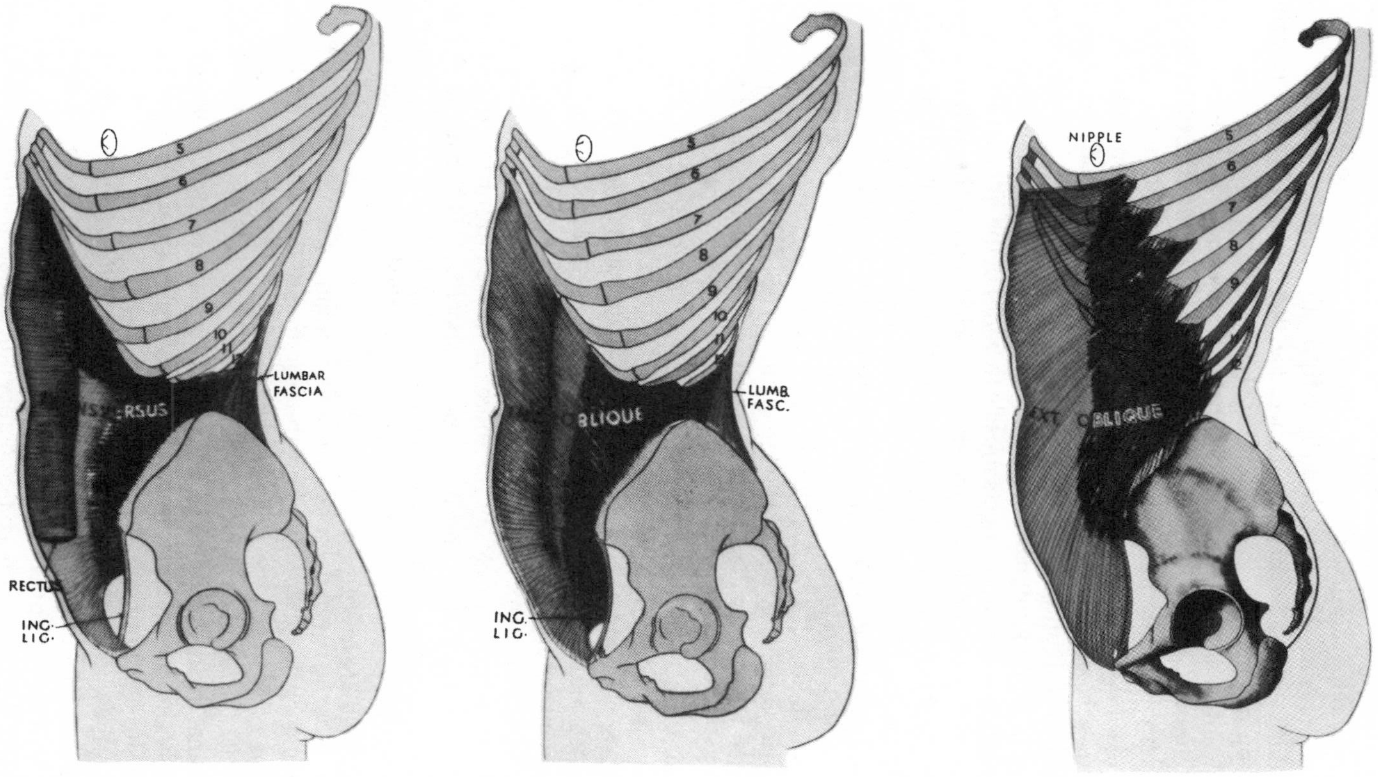

TRANSVERSUS ABDOMINIS   OBLIQUUS INTERNUS ABDOMINIS   OBLIQUUS EXTERNUS ABDOMINIS and forward. These muscles are the internal oblique and the external oblique muscles. Together, these three muscles largely determine the degree of abdominal compression (see Figures 2.7 and 2.8). They keep the trunk in a relatively fixed posture when the thoracic expiratory muscles begin to cóntract. The rate of airflow from the lungs is modified during phonation, especially in singing, because the respiratory tract is lightly closed by the glottis.

The internal oblique lies below the external oblique. Uppermost fibers of the internal oblique insert into the lower ribs and into the rib cartilages. The external oblique muscle is one of the most active muscles of the abdomen in delaying expiratory action through its natural antagonism with other muscles of the trunk. (It lies over the internal oblique.) Its fibers are attached to the ninth, tenth, and eleventh ribs, running downward and forward in an oblique manner (see Figure 2.8). A flat tendon, the aponeurosis (thick tissue that connects muscle to bone) of the internal oblique, the external oblique, and the transversus muscles, forms the anterior rectus sheath. It should be noted that the origins and the insertions of these muscles connect the region of the pelvis to the region of the sternum (see Figures 2.5 and 2.7). The large rectus abdominis (see Figures 2.3, 2.5 and 2.7), running from the pelvis to the sternum, is attached to the fifth, sixth, and seventh costals (ribs). (The nipple is located at the level of the fourth or fifth rib, relatively high in the torso, and serves as a point of topographic reference.) This muscular interplay can be seen in Figures 2.4, 2.5, 2.7 and 2.8.

The torso is generally symmetrical. The well-defined musculature of the torso is divided by a median tendinous topographic line, the linea alba, with observable muscular bands on either side (see Figure 2.7). Such well-developed muscle delineation should be the case with the tenor singer as with any other athlete.

Coordination among the abdominal muscles, the intercostal muscles, and the structural muscles of the thorax is needed for proper alignment of the axial body, that is, the head, neck, and trunk, so that the essential motor aspects of singing may occur efficiently. Control of these aerodynamic/myoelastic factors (what might subjectively be described as *breath energy in singing*) forms the foundation of all skillful singing.

In order to serve the long phrases of singing, the "shell of the torso," consisting of the abdominal and thoracic muscles, must be firmly developed so as to avoid the normal pattern of inward thoracic collapse that takes place as soon as spoken phonation begins. There must be no lower abdominal distention employed in attempting to counteract collapsing tendencies. The chest displacement observed in "normal" breathing is minimal in the well-trained singer.

A physical stability of the entire body, without rigidity, comes from proper axial alignment of head, neck, and torso. The appendages of the body, that is, the appendicular body comprising the arms, legs, and head (the head is part of both axial and appendicular structures), then have the freedom to move without disturbing the postural axis. Axial alignment ensures proper energization of the breathing mechanism.

THE *APPOGGIO* TECHNIQUE

Coordinated action among the muscles of the torso is expressed in the international school of singing as *la lotta vocale* (the vocal contest). This classic approach to breath management is not simply an extension of the normal breath cycle. It is a special method of managing the breath for the tasks of singing, in which the gesture of inspiration resists the gesture of expiration. In this way, sung phonation may be extended to ten, twelve, or even sixteen seconds, with subsequent silent breath renewal. During the *lotta vocale*, the upward movement of the diaphragm and the inward movement of the rib cage are retarded.

The *lotta vocale* accomplishes the *appoggio* technique of "breath support." The term *appoggio* derives from the Italian verb *appoggiare*, which means to lean, to lean against, to support, and to sustain. *Appoggio*, however, is not solely a breath coordination device. It includes the balancing of muscles and organs not directly associated with breathing. (For example, one speaks of *appoggio della nucca:* support of the nape of the neck.) The concept of *appoggio* includes actions that produce desirable resonance factors as well as efficient breath management.

The practical approach to learning *appoggio* technique begins with the postural considerations discussed earlier; *appoggio* depends upon axial alignment. The singer must first find the "noble posture" in which head, neck, and torso are in line with pelvic and hip regions; these focal points serve as the foundation for body alignment and permit freedom of movement in the appendicular body as well. Such posture can best be located by raising the arms straight upward over the head while inhaling silently and deeply. The arms are then brought back to the sides of the body while the chest remains in a relatively elevated posture, shoulders relaxed.

The noble posture may also be found by lying supine (almost always a book or pillow must be placed under the head to avoid chin and larynx elevation). One hand should be placed between the navel and the sternum, lightly touching the surface of the body, the other hand resting between the navel and the pelvis. A normal breath is taken through parted lips. (Avoid expansive breaths.) *Both inhalation and exhalation are completely silent.* There will be some outward motion in the epigastric-umbilical area (between sternum and navel) but little movement in the hypogastric (pubic) area between navel and pelvis. Of course, it is possible to pout out the lower abdomen locally when in this position, but such action has nothing to do with the actual breath cycle; by so doing, one is simply pushing in and out on the viscera. In fact, when the lower abdominal wall is forced outward, the costal area tends to move inward, thereby inducing more rapid lung volume reduction. This proves the fallacy of lower abdominal distention as a viable "breath support" method for singing.

In the supine position, one has an awareness of the alignment of head, neck, and torso, and of the stable position of the pectorals and the sternum. One experiences a slight outward movement of the abdominal wall, especially laterally, upon inspiration. This contact among the abdominal muscles can be maintained throughout most of the breath cycle; only near the close of the respiratory cycle will any inward motion occur in the wall. In the upright position, the same "noble" posture should be maintained, care being taken not to pull forcibly inward on the abdominal wall. This position, not necessary to the demands of speech, must be learned for the *appoggio* technique of breath management for singing.

Not until proper upright posture has routinely been achieved should a singer attempt breath-coordination exercises. A collapsed trunk prohibits *appoggio* management. Perhaps one of the most detrimental approaches to breath coordination is based upon false assumptions about "relaxation" during singing. Of course, muscle tension is to be avoided, but muscle *tonus* is vital to all energized physical action. Permitting the torso to slouch (under the illusion that the singer is then relaxed) is foreign to the *appoggio* system.

Assuming that the tenor has established good posture with proper structural support for the entire singing instrument (head to toes, with the weight of the body just in front of the arch of the foot, not on the heels), it is now time to move to specific exercises for the development of good breath coordination within this structure.

The key to elongating the breath cycle lies in the ability to sing short detached notes while silently replenishing the breath between them so that the muscles and organs of the trunk remain for extended periods of time quite near the inspiratory position (*la lotta vocale*). The large abdominal muscles (transverse, internal oblique, external oblique, and rectus abdominis) are thereby trained to avoid habitual immediate contraction following inhalation. The external intercostals do not make an early surrender to the internals. The sternum neither rises nor falls. The diaphragm descends more completely and ascends less rapidly. Breath expulsion is minimal in the short onset, and breath renewal takes place at the moment of termination of the brief phonatory event. *The new breath is the release of the phonation.*

The singer feels that the inner/outer abdominal muscular wall remains near the expanded, relaxed posture it had at the moment of inspiration, except for minute, quick umbilical/epigastric impulses at the moments of onset. This inward impulse is gently resisted internally, resulting in the *appoggio* phenomenon. Such internal/external muscular contact in the abdomen subjectively resembles what occurs when one places one hand over the other while keeping an easy, light balanced pressure between them. Practicing breath renewal while retaining muscular balance very much akin to that experienced at initial inhalation results in an extremely well-developed abdominal musculature.

The onset exercises that follow are precision exercises for coordinating the exact degree of the subglottic pressure with the sound intensity; airflow rate is then commensurate with the unconscious myoelastic (muscular) movements of the vocal folds.

As shown in Figures 2.9–2.13, subglottic pressure in the tenor voice during singing has been measured by means of an esophageal balloon; since pressure in the esophagus is similar to that in trachea and lungs, this is an accurate method for measuring changes in subglottic pressure.

The onset exercises recorded in Figures 2.9–2.13 were executed on a single pitch in the *zona di passaggio* at E_3 (165 Hz), with a lightly aspirated onset at moderate intensity. Slower-occurring onsets were at about the duration of one second. The termination of each phonation was the actual commencement of the subsequent breath renewal. (We recall the all-important *appoggio* adage: *the release is the new breath.*)

This process continues throughout subsequent exercises in which breath renewal becomes more frequent. It is precisely through the brief onset vocalise that the ability to maintain long phrases is eventually established.

In the short onset series, the muscles of abdomen and chest are schooled to maintain the antagonism necessary to *appoggio*. A feeling of muscular balance remains in the trunk, both laterally and dorsally—a feeling of light contact among the muscles of the abdominal wall. Breath renewal is absolutely silent and is indicated by the symbol [']. The singer scarcely realizes that breath is being renewed, feeling supraglottally as though remaining in the inspiratory gesture.

Figure 2.9 displays a series of vocal onsets using a quiet breath between voicings. It can be seen that subglottic activity creates a uniform pattern, only a small amount of air being used for each phonation. Most importantly, immediate and noiseless replenishment of breath takes place. The figure displays subglottic pressure and sound intensity in brief phonations of about a second's duration. The vibrato is apparent in the "sawtooth" figures; both the phonations and the silences between them are depicted.

The degree of regularity among the parameters in the other graphs (Figures 2.10–2.13) should be noted. Rapid onsets with exact regularity of release and onset as well as consistency of vibrato rate are visible in Figure 2.10, as are subglottic pressure and sound intensity values.

Figure 2.11 shows a rapid pattern of triplets with an inhalation occurring after each group of three short phonations rather than after each individual onset. Again, higher subglottic pressure corresponds to higher sound intensity; lower subglottic pressure corresponds to lower sound intensity. During moments of inspiration, a sudden glottal opening, with widely abducted vocal folds, ensures efficient breath renewal.

In Figure 2.12, a pattern of rapid sixteenth notes, with breath taken

FIGURE 2.9. Registration of esophageal pressure during repeated vocal onset of the vowel [e] at E_3 (167 Hz). Each phonation has a one-second interval.

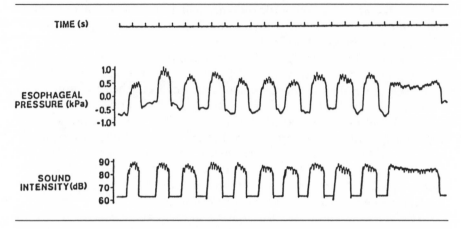

after each group of four notes, shows quick, silent inspiration that does not disturb the rhythmic consistency of the musical figure. In each inspiration the amount of air inhaled exactly meets the requirements of the subsequent four brief phonations. These exercises may be sung over an extended period of time. In executing them, airflow, vocal-fold approximation and breath renewal are precisely coordinated. This process is the long-established method of acquiring *appoggio* technique.

Figure 2.13 shows the same kind of activity, now with vowel change at each new sixteenth-note group. Notice that the subglottic pressure is in effect constant at each voicing. Because there is no time for conscious laryngeal adjustment, one may conclude that throughout the pattern the larynx neither rises nor falls, and that phonation begins with fully efficient

FIGURE 2.10. Registration of esophageal pressure during repeated vocal onset, with breath between phonations.

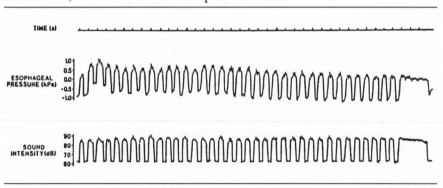

FIGURE 2.11. Registration of esophageal pressure during repeated vocal onsets, with breath after each triplet figure. A indicates high subglottic pressure and sound intensity; B indicates lower esophageal pressure and sound intensity; C indicates quick inspiration between triplet figures.

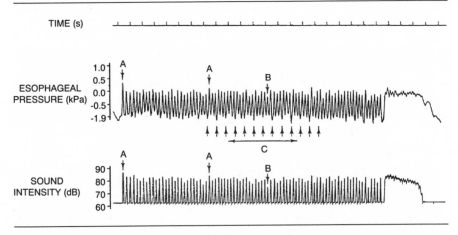

vocal-fold adduction, followed by precise abduction when the breath is renewed. The respiratory mechanism remains flexible, agile, and supple; the glottis opens and closes freely in response to the appropriate balance of

FIGURE 2.12. Registration of esophageal pressure during repeated vocal onsets; quadruples with breath renewal after each series. A indicates high subglottic pressure and sound intensity; B indicates lower esophageal pressure and sound intensity; C indicates quick inspiration between quadruples.

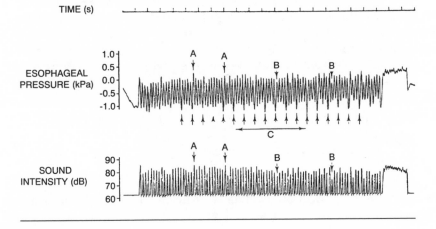

FIGURE 2.13. Registration of esophageal pressure during repeated vocal onsets; quadruples with vowel definition [i e ɑ ɔ], breath renewal before each vowel change.

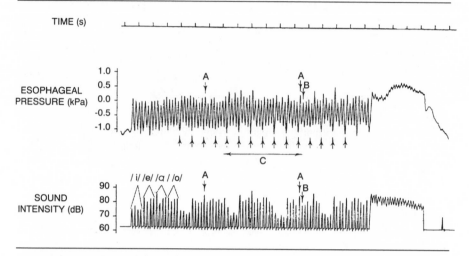

subglottic pressure, thereby avoiding all possibility of pressed phonation. Through these exercises the abdominal musculature is strengthened by remaining for long periods of time in the inspiratory position, which provides the foundation of the *appoggio* system of breath management.

ONSET EXERCISES

It is generally best to begin training this technical capability in lower middle voice on exercises constructed at about M.M. = 60 to the quarter note. With all exercises the teacher should supply underlying chordal accompaniments. Although the phonations of Figures 2.9–2.13 were executed on a single pitch, it may be more interesting to change pitches as indicated in Exercise 2.1. (Figure 2.12 is the result of a performance of Exercise 2.4.)

EXERCISE 2.1

After this precision onset exercise has been executed in a number of neighboring keys, with an awareness of flexible muscular contact in the abdominal wall, the singer should gradually increase the number and tempo of the detached onsets, as in Exercise 2.2 (recorded in Figure 2.10). The onsets in Figure 2.10 were performed at a sound duration of about half a second.

EXERCISE 2.2

The final whole note of Exercise 2.2 should be sung while remaining basically in the inspiratory posture that prevailed when shorter onsets were sung. Sternum and rib cage remain in a steady state (no chest displacement), as does the abdominal wall. It is not advocated that *no* movement occur in the abdominal wall. However, the small articulatory "bouncing" movement should be so minimal as to be barely perceptible.

The registration of rapid onset activity in Figure 2.10 is based on the pattern illustrated in Exercise 2.2. (The series in Figure 2.10 is twice as long as the pattern of Exercise 2.2.) The tenor working on this technique should gradually increase the number of detached onsets, breathing silently between them. In this fashion the exercises can easily be extended up to sixty seconds and longer. The abdominal wall and the rib cage, at the conclusion of each onset, remain almost exactly in the same position. There is a feeling of continued expansion in the lower trunk because the *appoggio* posture is being maintained.

In Exercise 2.3, which consists of a series of triplets, breath is taken after each group of triplets. Figure 2.11 illustrates that although the intake of air occurs only *after* each triplet figure, the glottis is freely parted for each of the three short phonations *within* the triplet figure. This means that the *appoggio* system develops freedom to release the glottis independently of inhalation.

EXERCISE 2.3

In Figure 2.12 and Exercise 2.4, the glottis parts after each detached note, then quickly re-engages for the subsequent note within the figure of four notes (quadruplets). *Inhalation, however, takes place only after each quadruplet.* As a result, the vocal folds separate (abduct) and engage (adduct) at a rapid rate, either with or without inhalation. The singer thus develops superb coordination between the muscles of laryngeal abduction and adduction and the muscles of respiration. During the moment of inspiration, a sudden glottal opening, with vocal folds widely abducted, ensures efficient inspiration and appropriate air supply for easy phonation in the subsequent series of onsets.

EXERCISE 2.4

The commencement of each phonation must exhibit vibrancy. The presence of vibrato (vibrancy) confirms that the neurological impulses that initiate vibrato—a relaxant maneuver involving the internal laryngeal muscles—are among the parameters of *appoggio* onset technique. Perhaps most significant, identical lung volume is established and maintained with the renewal of each breath regardless of the speed at which breath renewal takes place. (Even sophisticated studies of breath management frequently fail to take into account differences between breath management techniques in vocal pedagogy and often base conclusions on information derived from inefficient breath management systems.)

Figure 2.13 indicates the rhythmic patterns found in Exercise 2.4 but this time with a series of changing vowels. These patterns may be sung on any melodic sequence, as for example, the scale intervals 5–4–3–2–1, 1–3–5–8–5–3–1, or 1–3–5–3–1, in appropriate tonalities.

Fine tuning of airflow, subglottic pressure, sound intensity, glottal closure, and vibrato rate is established through the *appoggio* onset exercises. Onset exercises should be part of the daily technical routine of every tenor. The onset keeps the entire vocal mechanism conditioned. Coordination developed in the quick onset makes possible the extension of the *appoggio* to phrases of long duration, ensuring technical stability.

Scientific studies of breath management in rapid onsets (Richard Miller and Harm K. Schutte, 1985, *Folia Phoniatrica*) completely accord with the empirical language of historic *appoggio* pedagogy in its use of expressions such as "the release is the new breath," "stay in the position of singing while adding to your breath energy," "don't overcrowd the lungs, only satisfy them with the renewal of breath," "remain in the inspiratory posture as long as possible during each phrase," "sing on the gesture of inhalation," "do not induce exhalation by pulling in on the abdominal wall, but stay *ben appoggiato* (well supported)."

In accomplishing phrases of long duration while remaining *ben appoggiato*, several series of exercises that alternate short and long onsets are useful (Exercises 2.5–2.8). They should be executed at moderately slow tempos.

EXERCISE 2.5

EXERCISE 2.6

EXERCISE 2.7

EXERCISE 2.8

Exercise 2.9 illustrates a principle useful in developing the ability to breathe completely and silently in the short pauses often encountered between long cumulative phrases in the literature. A brief onset, or a series of them, is inserted in rhythmic fashion between long phrases.

EXERCISE 2.9

Tamino's aria ''Dies Bildnis'' (*Die Zauberflöte*) well illustrates the juxtaposition of phrases of brief and longer duration. Although there are several points within the aria where rests interrupt the melodic line, the aria is typical of the sustained singing at high *tessitura* so frequently met in the tenor operatic literature (see Examples 2.1 and 2.2).

EXAMPLE 2.1. From "Dies Bildnis ist bezaubernd schön," *Die Zauberflöte*, Mozart.

Operatic Anthology, Vol. III. Reprinted by permission of G. Schirmer, Inc. International copyright secured.

Exercises 2.10 and 2.11 may be accomplished phrase by phrase or as an entity. The following procedure is useful:

1. Sing the phrase on a front vowel such as [e]
2. Sing the phrase on a mixed vowel such as [œ]
3. Sing the phrase on a back vowel such as [o]

EXAMPLE 2.1. Continued

Operatic Anthology, Vol. III. Reprinted by permission of G. Schirmer, Inc. International copyright secured.

4. Sing the phrase on the vowels inherent in the text
5. Sing the original text, with inserted onsets during the originally notated rests.
6. Sing the original version of the phrase, omitting the inserted onsets.

Although this device may take some time, its efficacy is remarkable in solving breath-management problems in the literature.

EXERCISE 2.10

EXAMPLE 2.2.   From "Dies bildnis ist bezaubernd schön," *Die Zauberflöte*, Mozart.

Operatic Anthology, Vol. III. Reprinted by permission of G. Schirmer, Inc. International copyright secured.

EXERCISE 2.11

Any phrase in the literature is, of course, an exercise in breath management. It is a premise of the *appoggio* system that by training the musculature of the thorax and abdomen to resist the expiratory gesture, the singer develops the capability to sing long, cumulative phrases. However, all too often the tenor practices only long sustained phrases in the hope of increasing breath capacity. Even breath-holding exercises are sometimes advocated. Yet the purpose of breath-coordination exercises is not to learn to "hold" the breath but to engage successfully in the *lotta vocale* (the vocal contest), during which the inspiratory muscles do not immediately give up the "battle" to the expiratory muscles. Exercises intended to increase lung capacity or the ability to hold the breath are mostly useless. Total lung capacity is largely a fixed physiologic dimension in the mature singer. What is required is not a stretching of lung capacity but the ability to remain longer in the inspiratory period by regulating breath emission through efficient phonation. Trying to "hold" the breath induces harmful resistance at the vocal-fold level.

In summary, the tenor should be aware that breath management for singing requires a special breath coordination in which expiratory processes are delayed without increasing laryngeal action beyond the requirements of a specific phonation. Radiographic studies verify that in the *appoggio* technique of breath management, synergistic action between the muscles of respiration and the muscles of phonation is precisely coordinated.

Chapter 3

Vowel Modification ("Covering") in the Tenor Voice

The discussion concerning categories of tenor voices indicated that, generally, the higher the frequencies (pitches) at which *passaggi* events occur in the scale, the lighter the voice; the lower the *passaggi* events, the heavier and more dramatic the voice. Before the technical process often termed "covering" is examined, some qualifications regarding *passaggi* and vocal categories must be mentioned briefly.

There are baritones who have slightly smaller larynges and less dramatic voices than do some types of tenors, yet such baritones have *passaggi* points that occur lower in pitch than is the case with certain tenor instruments. Most baritones of this sort do not have voices of professional dimension and are not capable of performing operatic literature.

The lyric baritone has slightly higher *passaggi* points than does the dramatic baritone, just as the coloratura soprano's *passaggi* lie higher in the scale than those of the dramatic soprano. Similar phenomena of registration pertain, of course, among the several categories of the tenor voice. Physical differences determine how any particular singer should deal with the *zona di passaggio* (the area that lies between the two *passaggi*, i.e., the register pivotal points). It is in this middle voice (*voce media*) that controversy exists regarding "covering." The question is *when* and *how much* to "cover."

The term "covering" causes frequent confusion because it has too many possible connotations to convey a universally understood definition. The term *vowel modification* is a preferable expression.

PHYSICAL FACTORS

In some schools of vocal pedagogy (largely Germanic/Nordic), "covering" describes heavy mechanical action produced by conscious laryngeal depression, conscious spreading of the pharyngeal wall, excessive epiglottic lowering and, at times, pronounced narrowing of the laryngeal collar. (The laryngeal collar is a muscular ring consisting of the aryepiglottic folds that runs from the arytenoid cartilages to the sides of the epiglottis; it includes the arytenoids and the cartilages of Wrisberg. It defines the vestibule of the larynx, and the shapes it assumes affect resonance factors.)

In the historic international Italianate school *copertura* ("covering") describes *gradual* acoustic adjustments brought about through modifying vowels in the ascending scale. There is, however, no doubt that within this historic pedagogy, changes do occur in the velar region, in the pharyngeal wall, in epiglottic postures, in the ventricular (laryngeal sinuses) region, and in the region of the piriform sinuses. The question is one of the degree of conscious maneuvering.

The larynx is retained in the relatively low position it assumes upon inhalation, but without forced depression, and laryngeal elevation is avoided; there is no sudden "shifting of gears," no "hooking in" or "over," and no conscious muscular spreading in the pharynx, although there is a sense of openness in the pharynx. In several pedagogical orientations, the practice of "covering" lies somewhere between the two classic registration models exhibited by the Italianate and the Germanic/Nordic schools. Still, the less conscious effort involved in "covering," the better.

In schools with a typical Germanic orientation, *Deckung* (covering) requires sudden, heavy mechanical action in the laryngopharynx, as has just been described, whereas *copertura* (also known as *voce coperta*) of the Italianate school involves a process of vowel adjustment (*aggiustamento*) or vowel rounding (*arrotondamento*) that does not require major consciously induced changes at the level of the larynx and in the neighboring supraglottal regions. *Copertura* begins in the *zona di passaggio* (passage zone) as a gradual process of vowel migration. This *arrotondamento* technique achieves scale unification because the mouth gradually opens with rising pitch, just as it does for ascending pitch in calling or in laughter. This process of gradual "covering" is, then, best described in English as "vowel modification."

"Open" singing (*voce aperta*) is to be avoided in any range of the singing voice. "Closed voice" (*voce chiusa*) has nothing to do with throat posture. The term *voce chiusa* describes timbre that is not "open," in which the balance of upper and lower partials avoids shrill or dull quality. (Because of the possibility of undesirable connotations for English-speaking persons, it is preferable to substitute the expression *voce chiusa* for "closed voice." Vowel modification helps achieve *voce chiusa* through the entire scale; although modified, the vowel does not lose its basic definition except in highest frequencies, and can be distinctly perceived. In the traditional Germanic/Nordic school (which is by no means universally practiced by German and Nordic teachers) vowel definition is largely obliterated in much of upper range because of the supraglottal resonator distortion associated with notions of "cover."

The concept of vowel modification avoids the problems caused by the physical and acoustic adjustments that are necessary to sudden "covering." Gradual opening of the mouth alters relationships among harmonic partials of the spectrum, but the same postures of tongue, lips, and zygomatic (area of the cheeks) muscles are retained while defining the vowel. This natural phonetic process follows exactly the acoustic rubric that as the mouth opening increases, the upper formants uniformly lessen. In so doing, the singer avoids increasing the acoustic strength of upper partials as pitch mounts. Resonance adjustment then occurs as a natural process in the heightened expression that comes in sung phonations.

The neutral vowel [ə] is the central point for all vowel modification (see Figure 3.1). For example, the vowel [e] partakes of some neutralization

FIGURE 3.1. Some spoken vowel postures.

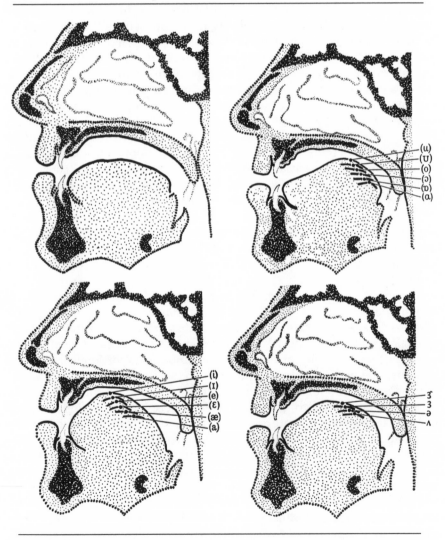

Phonetics, C. Kantner and R. West. New York: Harper & Brothers, 1960. By permission.

as it modifies toward the vowel [ε], that is, as it begins to approach the neutral vowel. This is the result of increased buccal (mouth) opening, as was just mentioned. In the same manner, the vowel [o] may modify toward the vowel [ɔ] as pitch ascends, or in certain other instances it may modify toward the vowel [U].

The principle of vowel modification is that the initial vowel undergoes some migration as the scale ascends, by modifying toward a near neighbor. The laryngeal configuration changes for each vowel, and there should be a corresponding change in the shape of the resonator tract. When the filtering aspects of the vocal tract are in tune with laryngeal configurations, the vowel is properly "tracked." Vowel modification in the ascending scale permits vowel tracking and balancing of the formants (areas of acoustic strength), thereby avoiding either "open" or heavily "covered" singing.

This system of vowel modification (*copertura*), which dates at least to the nineteenth century, is expressed in a schematic design in Figure 3.2. The extent of this *aggiustamento* varies with the *passaggio* events of the individual voice. But the need for vowel modification that avoids excessive mechanical laryngeal and pharyngeal adjustments in singing pertains for all voices, including all tenor categories.

As the tenor modifies a vowel toward its near neighbor, some adjustment of the upper harmonic partials that identify the vowel will take place. In this fashion, shrill sound, the "white" voice (*voce bianca, voix blanche*) associated with "open" vocal production is avoided. *Copertura* is especially necessary in the tenor voice because much demanding singing lies in the

FIGURE 3.2. Vowel modification chart. Several vowels and their neighbors are indicated.

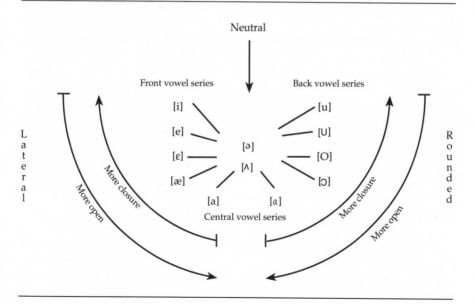

zona di passaggio and above the *secondo passaggio*. Although vowel modification is both an acoustic and a physical action, the mechanical changes are much less drastic in the *copertura* technique than in the "heavy and early cover" advocated in some vocal pedagogies. Further, *copertura* does not disturb vibrato rate, whereas in heavy "covering" the vibrato often will widen, or the tone will straighten out.

When a clearly defined vowel is modified, the resonance factor known as the *singer's formant* (see the chapter on tenorial resonance) must still be present if the vocal scale is to exhibit timbre uniformity. Although it may be too simplistic to say that proper *voce chiusa* throughout the singing voice automatically achieves appropriate degrees of opening and closing of all vowel sounds in an ascending scale, the trained ear discovers that desirable *voce chiusa* can exist only in conjunction with the process of *copertura*.

In a mounting scale, front close vowels usually modify "downward" toward a neighbor vowel, as indicated by the "more open" arrow in the schematic design of Figure 3.2. The modification process applies to the back vowel series as well. Whenever a singer has been taught to drop the jaw excessively, with resulting heavy production, modification to a less rounded neighboring vowel may be helpful. For example, at times the vowel [u] will need to modify to the vowel [U]; the [o] may be opened to [ɔ].

Above all, there is no single pitch in the mounting scale at which all vowels modify for all singers in uniform fashion, as is sometimes assumed. Although vocal *Fach* and the corresponding *passaggi* points dictate vowel modification, individual morphology must also be taken into consideration. In short, *copertura* is for one singer achieved by approaching the neutral vowel [ə] or the vowels on the back/rounded series, while for another singer *copertura* on the same pitch and vowel is induced by moving in the direction of the front/lateral group of vowels including [æ]. The cultivated musical ear determines which should occur, but acoustic analysis verifies the necessity for a balanced relationship between the lower and the upper harmonic partials. If an ascending (or descending) sung passage sounds spread or open, particularly through the *zona di passaggio* region, then greater closure toward a lateral vowel is required; if the sound is too narrow (too strong on upper partials associated with the lateral vowels), then more opening of the vowel toward the neutral or rounded series is demanded.

The epiglottis acts as a "lid" closing over the larynx during swallowing so that no food or foreign objects can enter the trachea (windpipe). (However, contemporary medical research indicates that it is possible to learn to swallow effectively even without normal epiglottic movement.) The epiglottis may also react to vowel differentiation, chiefly in response to tongue motion. One of the reasons the otolaryngologist, when using the laryngoscope (laryngeal mirror), requests that the patient repeat "ee!" ([i]) in falsetto is that on the vowel [i] the tongue is forward and the epiglottis does not obscure the vocal folds. With each change of vowel in the series [i e ɑ o u] the position of the epiglottis may change. Thus the epiglottis tends to play a role as vowel modification takes place toward either a front/lateral vowel or a back/rounded vowel. In a quite literal sense, vowel modification may be related to "covering" because during the progression from front to back vowels, the vocal folds become gradually obscured by motions of the base of the tongue and the epiglottis. These movements possibly contribute to the damping out of some upper partials from the laryngeally generated source of sound. There is, of course, for each vowel a different subconscious configuration within the larynx (as earlier mentioned) together with a corresponding shape of the vocal tract.

Each vowel has frequencies and amplitudes that correspond to resonances of the vocal tract. When one recites the vowel series [i e ɑ o u], pitch levels fall unless consciously inhibited through the speaker's raising them. Average values of formant frequencies of ten vowels may be seen in Figure 3.3. (Vowel formants are composed of the partials of a tone that determine the characteristic quality of each vowel.) Figure 3.4 shows a tabulation of the average first, second, and third formant frequency values in male and female voices as vowels change in speech.

In Figure 3.4 the second and third formants of [i] (ee) in a typical male speaking voice are at approximately 2290 Hz and 3010 Hz (although slightly higher in some tenor voices), while the neutral vowel [ə] shows 1190 Hz and 2390 Hz. As neutralization of a vowel occurs, upper harmonic partials lessen. (Opening the mouth reduces higher harmonic partials uniformly while strengthening the lower harmonic partials; keeping the mouth in a lateral position uniformly heightens upper partials.) When tenorial resonance is considered in Chapter 4, the role of the singer's formant, evident in the 2500–3300 Hz range for the typical *tenore lirico*, will be discussed.

Vowel modification in the traditional international school of vocalism begins almost imperceptibly at the *primo passaggio* (D_4 for the lyric tenor model) and is minimally increased on subsequent semitones until F_4 or $F_4^{\sharp}$ (depending in part upon the type of phrase being sung), by which point vowel modification has gradually taken place. (We recall that *voce media* for the lyric tenor lies between D_4 and G_4.) Then the resulting timbre at the G_4 register transition does not strike the ear as a sudden "flipping over" or "hooking in." In the *copertura* system of vowel modification, the singer experiences registration sensations without inducing extreme mechanical action. Sound may feel even more "in the head" during register transition, more compact, and proprioceptive frontal awareness may increase. There is a corresponding awareness of actively retaining the inspiratory posture (remaining *appoggiato*) earlier described. This is because along with the vowel modification essential to *voce chiusa* in the *passaggio* region, there must be an increase of breath energy in cooperation with proper laryngeal muscle responses (the appropriate glottal closure) previously discussed.

FIGURE 3.3. Average values of formant frequencies for 10 English vowels. The vowels were spoken in isolated single syllabic words.

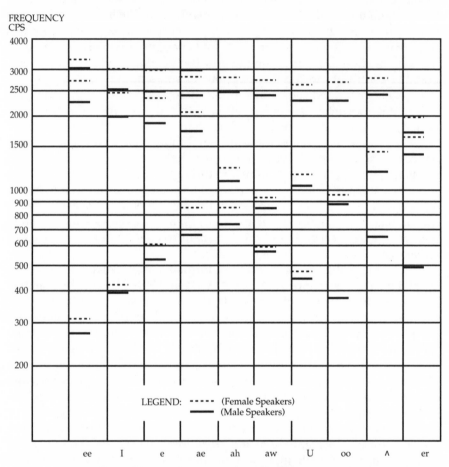

Average values of formant frequencies for 10 English pure vowels. The vowels were spoken in isolated single syllable words.

The Speech Chain: The Physics and Biology of Spoken Language, Peter Denes and Eliot Pinson. Philadelphia: Bell Laboratories (Dell Publishing), 1963. By permission.

Balanced vibrant timbre (presence of vibrato) substantiates this coordination.

Timbre concepts initiated by the trained musical ear demand and the body delivers, but only after the body has found the proper physiologic and acoustic pathways.

FIGURE 3.4. Tabulation of the average formant frequency values, in speech.

	ee	I	e	ae	ah	aw	U	OO	∧	er
First Formant Frequency										
Male:	270	390	530	660	730	570	440	300	640	490
Female:	310	430	610	860	850	590	470	370	760	500
Second Formant Frequency										
Male:	2290	1990	1840	1720	1090	840	1020	870	1190	1350
Female:	2790	2480	2330	2050	1220	920	1160	950	1400	1640
Third Formant Frequency										
Male:	3010	2550	2480	2410	2440	2410	2240	2240	2390	1690
Female:	3310	3070	2990	2850	2810	2710	2610	2670	2780	1960

The Speech Chain: The Physics and Biology of Spoken Language, Peter Denes and Eliot Pinson. Philadelphia: Bell Laboratories (Dell Publishing), 1963. By permission.

The principle of vowel modification may be illustrated in a passage from Handel's *Samson,* in which the text "all dark" first occurs in the speaking range of the singing voice, then is repeated as the phrase passes through *voce media* (see Example 3.1).

A tenor voice of sturdy proportions is appropriate to the role of Samson. A *lirico spinto* will sing the [ɑ] vowel of the word "dark," found on the lower pitch level, with nearly the same mouth position as encountered in speech, because the sung pitch is at speech level. The text repetition finds the vowel [ɑ] modifying slightly in the direction of [ɔ] for the ascent through $F_4^\sharp$ (the *lirico spinto secondo passaggio*). The vowel [I] in the second syllable of "amidst" on G_4 will be more "open" than if sung an octave lower, because the mouth must open for the increase in pitch and power. This, in effect, provides the necessary vowel migration in the direction of slight neutralization to ensure equalization of the mounting scale.

Later at E_4 (see Example 3.2), on the word "stars," the mouth will open more for that syllable than in lower voice, now shaping toward the vowel [ɔ]. Even more decisively, the vowel [ɑ] in the word "stars" at the climactic $F_4^\sharp$ modifies toward the neutral vowel [ʌ].

These *Samson* passages point out the need to adjust the degree of vowel modification to the requirements of each category of tenor voice.

EXAMPLE 3.1. From "Total Eclipse," *Samson*, Handel.

By permission, Boosey & Hawkes.

Modification that might be appropriate for the *spinto* instrument would be excessive for a lighter lyric voice. In every case, though, the vowel will undergo some modification as the mouth opens for ascending pitch. With certain tenors, it may seem that the $F_4^\sharp$ in this aria is more easily accomplished in "open" production than with the correct *copertura* of vowel modification; less actual energy may be involved in the more "open" sound. However, the balance between subglottic pressure and vocal-band action must not be slack, with resulting thin and disconnected timbre. The mounting scale demands some *aggiustamento* (modification) of the vowel.

Another example of the principle of vowel modification comes from the Schumann-Eichendorff *Liederkreis*, in the third song, "Waldesgespräch." The climactic passage "Es ist schon spät, es ist schon kalt" begins in *voce media* (middle voice) (that is, the *zona di passaggio*) and mounts on the vowel [I] to pitch levels above the *secondo passaggio*. If the singer is a light tenor, he probably will require little modification of the vowel even though it is a "high" front vowel; yet the mouth, in opening

EXAMPLE 3.2. From "Total Eclipse," *Samson,* Handel.

By permission, Boosey & Hawkes.

for pitch and power, will have modified the vowel [I] toward a greater degree of "openness" than would be found an octave lower (see Example 3.3).

If the tenor is a *lirico spinto,* the same vowel on the G$\sharp_4$ may modify in the direction of greater "openness" in order to match vocal timbre as the vowel emerges from the middle register. In the process, there will be changes in the supraglottic regions of the pharynx and in the larynx itself in response to vowel modification, but it should again be underscored that

EXAMPLE 3.3. From "Waldesgespräch," *Liederkreis*, op. 39, Schumann.

es ist   schon spät,   es   ist_____ schon kalt,

Sergius Kagen, ed., International Music Corporation. By permission.

they do not produce the heavy mechanical changes that would occur had early and excessive "cover" taken place on the preceding pitches. These desirable supraglottic events are also partly determined by airflow and subglottic pressure.

Perhaps the classic example of how vowel modification works in tenor voices may be illustrated by the traditionally performed (not originally written) C_5 passage from "Che gelida manina," Rodolfo's first-act aria from *La Bohème* (see Example 3.4). Were a tenor of any category to sing the "la speranza" phrase an octave lower than the indicated pitches, he would do so with mouth postures close to those used in speaking those syllables. An octave above, at performance pitches, the mouth opens for pitch and power but the basic forms of the vowels (with regard to lips, tongue, zygomatic area) are retained. The tenor continues to differentiate the vowels [a] and [e], but the modification process shows a spectral change toward [ɔ] and [ɛ], or even [æ]. By means of *aggiustamento*, formants are uniformly lowered so that the conjoining of high pitch and frontal vowel does not produce a shrill sound. The *chiaroscuro* (light-dark) quality resulting from the balanced spectrum is ensured through this process of *copertura*. (In Chapter 4 the matter of formants, resonance balancing, and the *chiaroscuro* is discussed in greater detail.)

In opposition to the gradual *aggiustamento* here being advocated, certain schools of singing begin "cover" suddenly and decisively at the first registration pivotal point (D_4 for the lyric tenor model). It becomes increasingly heavy in the *zona di passaggio*, so that by the time G_4 is reached, the vowel [a] may have become the vowel [U]. Such "covering" induces heavy action of the vocalis muscles. Heavy vocalis dominance does not permit the proper vocal-fold mass diminution that should occur during the vocal-fold elongation necessary for rising pitch. This heavy production also causes tensions in the vestibule of the larynx and excessive activity in the aryepiglottic folds (which extend from the arytenoid cartilages to the sides of the epiglottis). Resonance balance is directly altered by changes of shape in the laryngeal vestibule. The problem with the heavy mechanical action of too much "cover" too soon is that areas of the resonator tract are suddenly placed in static, nondynamic postures that inhibit flexible adjustment for vowel definition and frequency (pitch) changes. Aesthetically, such excessive "covering" is perceived as producing hard, rigid timbre that suffers from loss of vibrancy and brilliance. The purpose of vowel modification, "covering," or *aggiustamento* should be to reduce the increasing high rate of upper harmonic partials that would otherwise make those pitches and syllables shrill or open. "Cover," however, should not produce dull, wooden or hard sound, which is costly in both health and aesthetic results.

With a tenor who has been taught excessive "covering" through the *passaggio* zone (which is frequently the case), the teacher's task is to modify the vowels in that *tessitura* in the direction of front vowels. In the process, care must be taken to retain the *chiaroscuro* (bright/dark) timbre of the gradual *copertura* process. Resonance balancing in the *zona di passaggio* is the key to teaching the entire upper range of the tenor voice. In general, most young tenors of operatic potential "cover" the pitches F_4, $F_4^\sharp$, and G_4 excessively because they listen to mature professional voices that are larger and heavier than their own instruments. Or they may have been taught that male voices all "cover" at the same pitches (a misguided pedagogical theory still found in some quarters).

Much of the foregoing discussion is aimed at avoiding the heavy production that seems, at times, to flout the tenets of traditional vocal pedagogy. In contrast, some assumptions as to what constitutes "head voice" are as detrimental to vocal health as is heavy mechanical action. *Voce aperta* (open singing) is injurious and unaesthetic. Some vowel modification *must* take place between the first and second register pivotal points in order to permit an equalized scale and to ensure healthy production. *That which is physiologically and acoustically most efficient is most pleasing to the largest number of seasoned listeners.*

The best way to gain mastery over the degree of *copertura* is to isolate the *passaggi* in series of vocalises that approach pivotal registration points from several pitch directions on a variety of vowel changes. It is preferable to begin with a front vowel. (Front vowels are sometimes termed *high* vowels by singers, whereas vowels of the back vowel series are often called *low* vowels. Singers use the terms *high* and *low* because of proprioceptive responses to sensations created by sympathetic vibrations from the changing harmonic partials involved in vowel definition.) The choice of a front vowel such as [e] permits the vowel formant and the "singer's formant" (see Chapter 4) to complement each other as participants in balancing resonance.

Although it is chiefly the *secondo passaggio* point that often frustrates a tenor, the problem generally results from what has taken place just

EXAMPLE 3.4. From "Che gelida manina," *La Bohème*, Puccini.

below it, in upper middle voice. Registration and resonance balancing are co-equals in establishing the even scale. To work on one is to assist the other. (Chapter 4 deals specifically with the resonance factors of the tenor voice.)

VOWEL MODIFICATION EXERCISES

In the first group of exercises that follows, the tenor begins just below the *primo passaggio* with short intervallic patterns that gradually enter upper middle voice. It should be remembered that the speaking voice terminates its highest inflections (when not calling) at about the first registration point (*primo passaggio*). At this pitch level the mouth begins to open more than is the case in the normal speech range. Opening the mouth for singing is like opening the mouth for any expression requiring an increase in pitch and power. There is no need to dislocate the jaw in order to open the mouth. (See "Problems Related to the Hung Jaw," Chapter 7.) Nor should there be an exaggerated mouth opening at the *primo passaggio*. The expression on the face of the singer should appear pleasant and natural, and the differentiation of vowels prohibits the setting of the mouth or the jaw, either perpendicularly or laterally.

Vowel tracking, the flexible adjustment of the mouth and pharynx (i.e., the buccopharyngeal resonator system), is essential to the changing acoustic patterns that produce speech recognition. The same patterns pertain in the singing voice. "Si canta come si parla" (One sings as one speaks) may be an admonition sometimes misunderstood with regard to the need for increased energization in the singing voice, but in its relationship to vowel tracking, the historic adage contains much wisdom. It is supportive of all current acoustic verification and leads us directly to the most important pedagogical dictum regarding supraglottic factors in the singing voice: *There is no one ideal position of the mouth for singing; the vowel and the pitch determine the shape of the mouth.* The second most important rule derives from the first: *Vowel modification occurs as a natural result of opening the mouth for ascending pitch and power.* These two fundamental rules should be adhered to in executing the vocal exercises that follow.

Passaggio exercises should be interspersed with exercises devoted to other technical aspects of singing, such as onset and agility. They should be used *only* after the voice is well warmed up.

Exercise 3.1 should first be sung on any single vowel from the front vowel series, such as [e], at a moderately slow tempo. (In the case of a young tenor who finds the exercise strenuous, it should be truncated so as to avoid the higher keys.)

EXERCISE 3.1 AND 3.2

Exercise 3.2 uses the same musical pattern as Exercise 3.1. However, a change from a "high" vowel to a "low" vowel takes place on the upper pitch of each phrase. Mouth shapes change in accordance with the requirements of vowel definition and register adjustment. Below are suggested combinations of vowel changes:

[e]–[ɔ]
[e]–[o]
[e]–[u]

In the second musical pattern (Exercise 3.3), the tenor begins at, or near, the *primo passaggio*, descends by a brief pattern, then re-ascends. Once again a front-series vowel is recommended.

EXERCISE 3.3 AND 3.4

Exercise 3.4 uses the same musical pattern as does Exercise 3.3. The change from front to back vowel ("high" to "low") takes place on the second bar of each phrase. Suggested combinations of vowel changes are

[e]–[ɔ]
[e]–[o]
[e]–[u]

Exercise 3.5 lies within the passage zone (*zona di passaggio*). The first half of the exercise begins below the *primo passaggio*, rises to the *zona di passaggio* region, then descends by passing tones. The second half of the exercise begins in the upper region of the *zona di passaggio* and reverses the process.

EXERCISE 3.5

The following series of exercises should be adjusted upward or downward for lighter or heavier tenor instruments. They begin below the *primo passaggio* and progress through the passage zone to the area of the *secondo passaggio*. Suggested vowels are indicated, but other front vowel/back vowel patterns may be substituted.

EXERCISE 3.6

The pattern of Exercise 3.6 should then be sung with a change of vowel, [e] to [ɔ], at the uppermost pitch (the 6th of the scale) (Exercise 3.7). In the return to a single back vowel (Exercise 3.8) the same resonance balance should be kept.

EXERCISE 3.7

EXERCISE 3.8

Thereafter, the musical patterns of Exercises 3.6, 3.7, and 3.8 should be raised to the key of A major, so that F$_4^\sharp$ becomes the point at which vowel change occurs. The sequence of the vowel [e], the change from [e] to [ɔ], and the execution of the single vowel [ɔ] should be carefully observed. The goal is to keep the same resonance balance throughout. Exercise 3.7 can profitably use other vowel combinations (e.g., [i] and [u]).

The next step is of major importance in the *copertura* technical system because of the crucial nature of the F$_4$–G$_4$ relationship (the bridge note is now F$_4$, and the *secondo passaggio* registration pivotal point remains G$_4$, in the *tenore lirico*). The three parts of the series may be practiced independently. The entire series may be executed with the complete set of alternating front/back vowels, followed by back/front combinations. (Exercise 3.9)

EXERCISE 3.9

An important part of securing the *copertura* technique is to proceed to pitches immediately above the *secondo passaggio*, using various vowels. (Exercises 3.10, 3.11, 3.12)

EXERCISE 3.10

EXERCISE 3.11

EXERCISE 3.12

Over a period of weeks (perhaps months), teacher and tenor work on achieving timbre unification on these patterns, using keys that are concentrated in the *zona di passaggio*. As soon as the singer is comfortable with these, he moves to a neighboring key or keys. With each change of key the transitional pivotal point will have a different position within the scale.

In the key of C, for example, the pitch that may require most attention will be the third of the triad, E_4, both in approaching G_4 and in returning from it. Naturally, the G_4–A_4 interval must be realized completely in *voce piena in testa* timbre, maintaining a complete timbre match in the *zona di passaggio*.

Not infrequently, E_4 exhibits better timbre in *descending* from G_4 than in *ascending* to G_4. Then the singer should return to the descending triad (G_4–E_4–C_4), being certain the same "mixture" is present on E_4. Immediately thereafter, he should sing the reverse direction (C_4–E_4–G_4) of the triad, being certain that the two E_4 pitches share exactly the same timbre (Exercise 3.13).

EXERCISE 3.13

When the tenor negotiates with ease the previously indicated key, Exercise 3.13 should be transposed gradually upward by half steps.

Other valuable devices for ironing out the *passaggio* area and thereby achieving *copertura,* are exercises that omit notes of the triad and use octave intervals to progress upward and downward by semitones.

Exercise 3.14 is an example of an *aggiustamento* exercise. This kind of exercise should be reserved for tenors who already possess some skill in negotiating upper-middle and upper ranges.

EXERCISE 3.14

Exercise 3.14 may be profitably altered to accommodate vowel changes, as indicated in Exercise 3.15. As skill increases, these exercises may be transposed upward by semitones through the keys of A, B♭, and B. (Clearly, the higher *tessitura* of those keys should be reserved for the more accomplished tenor.)

EXERCISE 3.15

Another exercise often works well for the young tenor in his learning to enter the legitimate head voice (*voce piena in testa*) of upper range. It is based on a series of seventh chords in which the *zona di passaggio* pitches are first treated at the top of an arpeggiated pattern that originates in middle voice (Exercise 3.16).

Exercise 3.16 may be executed on a single vowel, or with vowel change on each arpeggiated portion of the exercise.

EXERCISE 3.16

In the key of G, the pitches $F_4^\sharp$ and $F_4^\natural$ are sung with appropriate vowel modification to produce timbre that matches the other notes in the arpeggiated figure.

In the key of $A^\flat$, the pitches G_4, $G_4^\natural$, and F_4 are the important points at which to secure matching timbre (Exercise 3.17).

EXERCISE 3.17

Following successful accomplishment in the keys of G and $A^\flat$, the tenor extends the same pattern to the keys of A, $B^\flat$, and B, with corresponding semitones above the *secondo passaggio,* following the rules of vowel modification. (The mouth will open as the *secondo passaggio* is approached, and this buccal aperture will slightly increase with each semitone above the *secondo passaggio*; however, the basic postures of the tongue and the lips maintain the integrity of the initial vowel, although the mouth is opening. Natural vowel modification [*aggiustamento*] alters the harmonic spectrum. Perhaps it is not amiss to recall here that vowel modification ensures that the conjoining of high pitch with front-vowel formants and the singer's formant will not produce excessive brilliance, which would be the case without modification.)

There remains one major device for *passaggio* work in the tenor voice. It consists of an arpeggio over the span of a tenth, at first with a vowel change only on the tenth, as in Exercise 3.18.

EXERCISE 3.18

Soon thereafter, the same pattern should be sung with alternating vowels from the front and back vowel series (Exercise 3.19). In all cases, other contrasting vowels, in addition to those indicated, may be used.

EXERCISE 3.19

Standard running scale patterns and arpeggios also serve for work on the *aggiustamento* of the extended range. (Sometimes the term *arrotonda-mento* is used interchangeably with *aggiustamento*, but *arrotondamento* is more accurately used to describe the rounding effect, acoustically, of the vowels [ɔ], [o], [ʊ], and [u] in the vowel modification process.)

Building the upper tenor range should not be hurried. It seldom can be won immediately, and often must be worked half-step by half-step. However, exercises such as the groups suggested above are designed to bring about proper adjustment (modification) of the vowel within the mounting scale in such a fashion as to accord with the historic *copertura* technique. The differences among the several categories of tenor will determine the extent of modification necessary to each vowel. The musicianly ear learns to listen for equalized timbre throughout the two-octave scale, thereby avoiding sudden changes in vocal color.

A number of examples from the literature serve well as exercises for achieving *copertura* in upper range. An excellent passage comes from the Gilda/Duca duet, *Rigoletto* (see Example 3.5). The segment begins for tenor just below the *primo passaggio* and progresses by half-step intervals through the *secondo passaggio*, mounting to B♮₄. As a practice device, the tenor may wish first to sing all twelve bars on a front vowel, such as [i], [e], or [ɛ], subsequently on a back vowel, such as [ɔ], [o], [ʊ], or [u], and then on a "mixed" vowel, such as [œ] or perhaps [y]. Next, the inherent vowels in the text are sung, without consonants, and finally the complete text is sung. This five-step process should be done one phrase at a time, as was earlier suggested with the *Zauberflöte* aria.

The phrase "donna celeste, d'invidia agli uomini sarò per te" is difficult to surpass as an exercise in *aggiustamento* for tenor voice. As pitch ascends, the tenor has the advantage of the "high" front vowel [i] introducing the "low" back vowels [ɑ] and [ɔ], followed by a return to the vowel [e] for the B♮₄. Thereafter, the vowel [i] leads to several syllables built upon other "open" vowels. This is masterful writing for the tenor instrument.

Another fine *zona di passaggio* vocalise comes from the third-act entrance of Rodolfo, *La Bohème* (see Example 3.6). This passage may be turned into a five-part exercise in exactly the same manner as has been suggested with Example 3.5.

The nine bars progress through *voce media*, contrasting front and back vowels. As did Verdi in the *Rigoletto* fragment cited, Puccini here sets front vowels on pitches in upper range. There is little doubt that both composers understood acoustic factors favorable to the tenor voice.

Other passages from favorite tenor arias show similar awareness of favorable textual treatment as *voce media* mounts into upper range. An example comes from Bizet's *Carmen*, in the aria "La fleur" (see Example 3.7). The composer leads the tenor stepwise through the *zona di passaggio*, not unlike what Verdi often does. The phrase "Et j'étais une chose à toi!", with the first half of the phrase consisting of front vowels leading to the more central vowel in "toi," serves as a classic vocalise for tenor voice.

Finally, the last phrase of "Ingemisco" (Verdi *Requiem*) provides an

EXAMPLE 3.5. From "È il sol dell'anima," *Rigoletto*, Verdi.

By permission of G. Schirmer, Inc. International copyright secured.

example of great writing for the tenor voice. It utilizes the juxtaposition of front and back vowels placed very favorably for tenor voice, as the phrase hovers in the *zona di passaggio*, mounting to a climactic $B^\natural_4$. At the phrase's initiation, "statuens" on $E^\flat_4$, Verdi chooses the register pivotal point (G_4). Thus he prepares the $A^\flat_4$ on the first syllable of "*par*-te" with two preceding "high" vowels. The phrase, from $B^\flat_3$ to $B^\natural_4$ on "me sequestra, statuens in parte dextra," is an unbeatable example of the accommodation of favorable vowel structure to the full potential of the tenor instrument coupled with musical and emotional heights (see Example 3.8). (Clearly, none of these operatic passages should be attempted except by mature singers who already possess substantial technical skills. They are for the emerging artist and the established professional.)

EXAMPLE 3.6. Third-act entrance, Rodolfo, *La Bohème*, Puccini.

Reprinted by permission of G. Schirmer, Inc. International copyright secured.

PEDAGOGICAL USES OF *FALSETTO* AND *VOCE FINTA*

Falsetto

In the late-teenage tenor voice, it sometimes seems that all attempts to enter upper voice in *voce piena in testa* (full legitimate "head voice") are unrewarding. In such cases, the young tenor should begin with a *falsetto*

EXAMPLE 3.7a. From "La fleur," *Carmen*, Bizet.

Operatic Anthology, Vol. III. Reprinted by permission of G. Schirmer, Inc. International copyright secured.

tone on a pitch that lies a few semitones below the *secondo passaggio,* in the *zona di passaggio,* and then pass from falsetto to legitimate voice on the same pitch.

This is not an exercise in blending falsetto into the rest of the voice with a view to introducing falsetto into public performance, a futile practice that stems from a misunderstanding of the physiologic events of falsetto. Rather, this is an exercise in which the singer immediately progresses from an onset in falsetto to legitimate *voce di testa* timbre. The purpose of the exercise is to avoid the laryngeal muscle-setting that sometimes accompa-

EXAMPLE 3.7b. From "La fleur," *Carmen*, Bizet.

Oma Carmen! et je'tais u_ne chose à toi! Carmen, je
O my Carmen! And I lived on-ly yours to be! Carmen, I

colla voce pp a tempo

t'ai - - - me!
love you!

pp colla voce ppp
a tempo

Operatic Anthology, Vol. III. Reprinted by permission of G. Schirmer, Inc. International copyright secured.

nies attempts to sing beyond the speech range (one assumes here a young tenor early in his technical training). The move from falsetto to full voice must be rapid, *without pause* (Exercise 3.20). With fairly sizable voices there will be an audible timbre change in the shifting from falsetto to legitimate voice; this is in no way undesirable.

EXERCISE 3.20

falsetto - voce piena

The exercises should be continued by semitone progressions on the pitches of the *zona di passaggio*. If there is evidence of vocal effort, or if weariness follows these attempts, the young tenor should stop. At a later practice session or lesson, he returns to those pitches that can be executed without strain from falsetto to full. It is important to increase the range on which these patterns can be sung, but only after step-by-step mastery.

EXAMPLE 3.8. From "Ingemisco," *Requiem*, Verdi.

Used by permission of C. F. Peters Corporation.

Sometimes the falsetto/full exercises are equally useful above the *secondo passaggio* (G$_4$ for the lyric), and with some tenors may be extended with comfort up through B$^\flat_4$, B$_4$, and even C$_5$ (especially with lyric instruments). This depends, again, upon the weight and category of tenor voice. Any time the practice of moving from falsetto to full voice (*voce piena in testa*) begins to produce either strain or by-noises (raspiness), it should be abandoned. In some cases it is highly successful, in others less so.

The same pedagogical reasons suggest another vocalise that brings good results in avoiding pressed phonation on the onset. As with Exercise 3.20, it is *not* the purpose of Exercise 3.21 to incorporate falsetto timbre into the *voce completa* (complete voice) that occurs in *voce piena in testa* timbre, the quality of tenor timbre that sounds "legitimate." The falsetto onset is utilized solely as a pedagogical device for avoiding any tendency toward pressed muscular onsets. As was previously mentioned, the intrinsic laryngeal muscle activity that produces falsetto (the imitation of female vocal timbre by the male) is not the same phenomenon as male "head-voice" function. Factors of vocal-fold elongation are present in the falsetto but with reduced activity of the vocal-fold closure mechanism. Therefore, in some cases, treating the falsetto as a kind of grace note to pitches that lie in the *zona di passaggio,* or even higher, removes the tendency of the overly athletic tenor to make a rigid presetting of the laryngeal and respiratory musculatures.

Exercise 3.21 is in three parts. They should be executed sequentially. The same admonitions regarding the use of Exercise 3.20 pertain here. All of these exercises are to be limited to a few minutes per practice session.

EXERCISE 3.21

Other falsetto exercises may be useful in bringing about greater freedom at the onset of sound and in subsequent phrases. The following exercises have the advantage of starting in upper voice, where some tenors have excellent falsetto facility. The procedure is to sing a reinforced falsetto (at a fairly high energy level that reduces the falsetto glottal chink somewhat) in a descending passage, changing to *voce piena in testa* either on the *passaggio* pivotal point itself (G_4 for the *tenore lirico*) or on neighboring notes below. Whereas Exercises 3.20 and 3.21 may be more appropriate to lighter categories of tenor, Exercises 3.22 and 3.23 often prove of greater assistance to heavier tenor voices.

EXERCISE 3.22

EXERCISE 3.23

These exercises may be transposed to neighboring keys as is appropriate for the individual tenor voice. The movement from falsetto to complete voice should eventually be practiced on all the pitches in the *zona di passaggio*.

In a case where an individual tenor has limited facility in using a descending falsetto timbre, falsetto on an ascending pattern beginning just below the *primo passaggio* may be helpful. Following the transition from falsetto to *voce piena in testa* (indicated in Exercise 3.24 on the pitch of the fermata), the tenor should repeat the transitional note as the first note of a descending arpeggio in full voice. The exercise can be extended upward by semitones.

EXERCISE 3.24

In all of these falsetto exercises, tenor and teacher should make use of changing vowel sequences. Then the most favorable vowel for the individual singer should be utilized. Falsetto exercises are intended only for those voices with tension problems in the *zona di passaggio*. With the exception of occasional effects in the *tenorino* and *leggiero* literatures, or for comic purposes, falsetto has no place in performance. It can be useful at times, in rehearsals, for "marking." (For comment on problems that may arise from reliance on falsetto, see Chapter 7.)

Voce finta

Voce finta is best translated as "feigned voice." It is also related to a timbre described in some German-speaking pedagogical circles as *Fistelstimme* (although that term is confusingly used to describe several kinds of timbre). *Voce finta* is a vocal timbre that sometimes is mistaken for falsetto. However, in *voce finta* the vocal bands are more completely occluded than in falsetto production. This timbre is achieved by reducing breath energy from pitches that require greater energization in *voce piena* timbre. *Voce finta* is not *mezzavoce* (which is piano singing with timbre characteristics of *voce piena* present), as Francesco Lamperti made clear in his undated *A Treatise on the Art of Singing*, from the 1860s:

> *Piano* should in all respects, with the exception of intensity, resemble the *forte*. It should possess with it in equal degree, depth, character, and feeling. It should be supported by an equal quantity of breath, and should have the

quality of tone, so that even when reduced to pianissimo it may be heard at as great a distance as the *forte.* (p. 17)

In contrast to the piano dynamic a tenor can produce in *voce piena in testa* (full voice, in the sense of *complete* voice), *voce finta* is achieved by diminishing the degree of breath energy, producing changes in the perception of depth, character, and feeling. *Voce finta* timbre can seldom be readily accomplished above the *secondo passaggio* because of the need for increased energy in both subglottic pressure and laryngeal muscle balance in singing the upper range with normal resonance balancing. It might be argued that *voce finta* is not a vocal register but a vocal coloration, a conscious violation of some registration principles that produce *voce completa* in upper middle voice.

Functionally, corresponding configurations in the supraglottal area distinguish *voce finta* from both *voce piena in testa* (which appears to have more complete vocal-fold closure) and falsetto (which has less complete vocal-fold closure). *Voce finta* is often produced by a slight head and chin elevation. This raises the larynx somewhat and thereby shortens the vocal

EXAMPLE 3.9a. From "Una furtiva lagrima," *L'Elisir d'amore,* Donizetti.

Operatic Anthology, Vol. III. Reprinted by permission of G. Schirmer, Inc. International copyright secured.

tract. The result is a distinct timbre change—a lighter and often slightly breathy quality.

Nevertheless, *voce finta* is a useful expressive device within the whole tenor palette of vocal sounds. It provides optional coloration to legitimate *mezzavoce* for emotive purposes. It tends to serve the same coloration purposes that falsetto sometimes is asked to perform, but *voce finta* can be incorporated directly into *voce di testa* whereas falsetto mostly cannot, except in the lightest of tenor categories. If, while executing *voce finta*, the head and laryngeal postures are returned to an axial position, *voce finta* can be crescendoed to *voce completa*. *Voce finta* is a timbre characterized by a certain sweetness and plaintiveness.

A perfect example of the effective use of *voce finta* in conjunction with other vocal colors of the tenor voice may be found in "Una furtiva lagrima" from *L'Elisir d'amore*. In the first four bars of the vocal line, which lie chiefly in the passage zone, the *dolce* character of the musical and dramatic writing makes *voce finta* an appropriate coloration; its execution is secure in this range (see Example 3.9a.) (As noted above, *voce finta* often is not successful above the *secondo passaggio*.) Beginning with bar 5 of the vocal line, "quelle festose giovani" (see Example 3.9b) should move into *complete* voice at

EXAMPLE 3.9b. From "Una furtiva lagrima," *L'Elisir d'amore,* Donizetti.

Operatic Anthology, Vol. III. Reprinted by permission of G. Schirmer, Inc. International copyright secured.

piano level to accommodate the mounting line and the accent on "fe-*sto*-se." Beginning with the word "invidiar," the singer may sing the F_4 in a "complete" *mezzopiano,* the next few notes again in *voce finta,* then finish the phrase in *voce mista* (the quality in which traditional pedagogy believes "head" and "chest" are appropriately mixed, designated by a number of voice teachers as a separate register.)

In the six-bar passage (see Example 3.9c) beginning with "Che più cercando io vo?", legitimate piano is required because of the increasing emotive nature of music and text. It will also be necessary to make use of *voce piena in testa* (complete [not loud] voice in head) timbre for the forthcoming crescendo during the sustained F_4 on the syllable "vo?" as it moves into the syllables "M'ama." It would be technically disastrous for most tenors to attempt the subsequent phrase "sì, m'ama" in *voce finta*; that timbre also would give the wrong dynamic level (*forte* is marked) and the wrong emotional color for such an impassioned expression. However, the last "lo vedo" can be extremely effective when begun in legitimate *mezzavoce,* proceeding to *voce finta,* especially at the embellishment and for the phrase conclusion.

A tenor who is skilled in the use of *voce finta,* who controls the piano dynamic in *voce mista,* and who is able to crescendo to the fuller dynamic

EXAMPLE 3.9c.   From "Una furtiva lagrima," *L'Elisir d'amore,* Donizetti.

Operatic Anthology, Vol. III. Reprinted by permission of G. Schirmer, Inc. International copyright secured.

possibilities in the *zona di passaggio* can bring about a musical and emotional effect of great beauty throughout the aria. For example, beginning the phrase "per poco a' suoi sospir!" in *voce finta* (to match the pianissimo *smorzando* marking), moving into a slightly higher dynamic level with more kernel to the sound as occurs in legitimate *piano* singing, then building to a more climactic and expressive level at "Cielo" and for the concluding traditional cadenza, the singer will have used many of the colors of his vocal palette (see Example 3.9d).

EXAMPLE 3.9d. From "Una furtiva lagrima," *L'Elisir d'amore,* Donizetti.

EXAMPLE 3.9d.   Continued.

spir...   Cie - lo, si può   mo - rir,   di più non
heart!   Af - ter that mo - ment fond   I   will die

chie - do, non chie   -   do   ah!
glad - ly, die glad   -   ly,   Ah!

Operatic Anthology, Vol. III. Reprinted by permission of G. Schirmer, Inc. International copyright secured.

In addition to its possibilities as a coloristic device, *voce finta* may be useful pedagogically, particularly for tenors who tend to grip (press) onsets and sustained phrases in upper-middle voice but who cannot easily produce falsetto in that range. As with falsetto, *voce finta* should never become a permanent substitute for proper negotiation of the even scale through the *zona di passaggio* (*voce mista*) region.

Voce finta timbre, especially in light categories of tenor voice, may be substituted for the falsetto quality in Exercises 3.20, 3.21, and 3.24. In fact, with some light tenors, *voce finta* proves more productive in those exercises than does falsetto. Singers with a tendency to under-energize the singing voice in the passage zone should avoid using *voce finta* as a pedagogical aid. Tenors who lack skill in bridging so-called "chest" and "head" often mistakenly rely upon the detached *voce finta* timbre to the detriment of proper access into *voce piena in testa* registration. They must understand that for them *voce finta* is a crutch to be thrown away.

Chapter 4

Tenorial Resonance and How to Achieve It

ACOUSTIC FACTORS

Singers often speak of "resonance," by which they mean a good balance of the acoustic factors that determine vocal quality. They also have in mind a vocalized sound that projects well over an orchestra in a large hall. Many assumptions as to how one achieves such resonance in the singing voice are based upon myths regarding "resonance chambers" and "sounding boards" that mysteriously lodge in the head or chest. Attempts to "place" the tenor voice sometimes result in impairment of balanced vocal timbre because they have no basis in fact. Sensation is often mistaken for source.

The vocal tract, the resonator tube of the voice, extends from the internal laryngeal area to the lips. It acts as a filter for sound initiated at the larynx. The vocal tract consists of the area lying immediately above the true vocal folds (supraglottic region), the ventricles (or sinuses) of the larynx (also known as the ventricles of Morgagni; these are adjustable spaces between the true and the false vocal folds), the pyriform (also piriform) sinuses, the vestibule of the larynx, the pharynx, the mouth, and the nose when it is not closed off from the rest of the resonating system through velopharyngeal action.

Assumptions about chest resonation, as well as head resonation (particularly the forehead and the frontal sinuses), for the most part belong to the mythologies that abound about the singing voice. Singers rely on sensation in singing, as they should; they do not need to know in detail the physiologic or acoustic sources for resonance sensation, but they should not naively try to induce responses in areas of the body where such responses cannot be generated.

As with any other instrument, the singing voice is composed of complex tones of more than a single frequency, the components of which are based on the overtone series. The singing voice has the potential to be rich in such overtones. The lowest frequency, the fundamental, is perceived as the pitch of the tone. The other frequencies are multiples of the fundamental and are known as harmonic partials. Depending mainly on vowel and pitch, certain partials carry more acoustic energy than do others. For this reason, the sound spectrum of the singing voice is characterized by a distribution of acoustic energy that supplies more strength to some resonance frequencies than to others. The regions in the spectrum where acoustic peaks are found are called *formants*.

The description of vowel modification in Chapter 3 noted that in speech there is heavy concentration of acoustic energy in the formant regions that define vowel structure (see Figures 3.3 and 3.4). In the singing voice, vocal-tract construction tends to produce three, four or five prominent formants that determine vocal quality. Changing the shape of the resonating tube—the vocal tract—changes relationships among the acoustic energy peaks. In practice, what one does with lips, mouth, jaw, tongue, velum, and pharynx radically influences the sound, no matter what the larynx may be "saying." There should be a natural phonetic selection, by the resonator tube, of sound produced at the larynx. Feedback from the shapes of the resonation system directly influences laryngeal action. These events clearly parallel theories of the phonetic source of speech intelligibility and correspond to the historic pedagogical notion previously mentioned: "Si canta come si parla."

When the singing voice demonstrates what singers call "ring," "ping," "focus," or "forward placement," a region of acoustic energy exists beyond most vowel formants produced in speech. This energy peak, which is not produced in quiet speech, is called the *singer's formant*. Spectral analysis shows it is located in the region of 2500–3300 Hz in a well-trained *tenore lirico* (see Figure 4.1).

FIGURE 4.1. Spectral analysis of the vowel [ɔ] sung at approximately 277 Hz (C♯₄). The spectral envelope indicates desirable vowel definition, the *first formant* and the *singer's formant*.

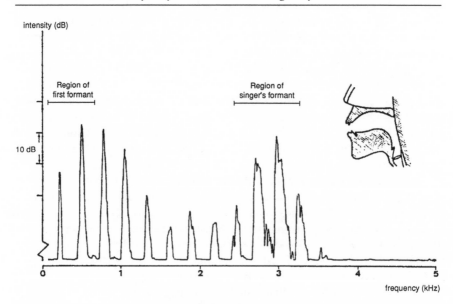

Spectral analysis of the singing voice also shows that a formant is consistently found in the lower portion of the spectrum in the region of 500 Hz. This formant represents depth or roundness in the sound. It is referred to as the *first formant* (see Figure 4.1).

The set of power spectra in Figure 4.2 shows that, in spite of their

FIGURE 4.2. Power spectra of vowels [i], [e], [ɑ], [o] and [u] at B♭₃ (233 Hz) and E♭₄ (311 Hz).

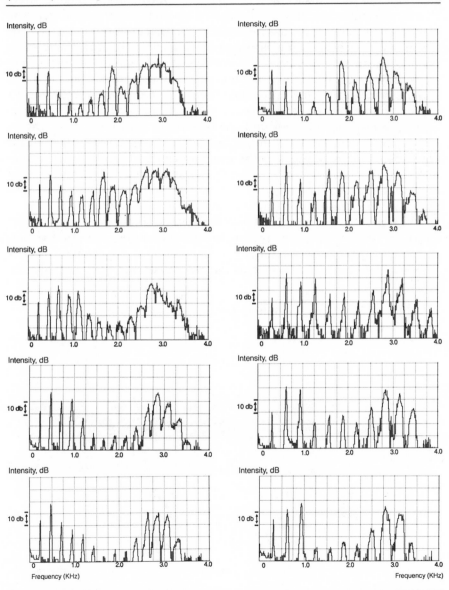

similarity at the top and bottom of the spectrum, vowels look different from each other in the middle of the spectrum. The front vowel [i] has acoustic strength in the upper part of the spectrum, near the region of the singer's formant; the front vowel [e], at a somewhat lower position in the spectrum; the more neutral vowel [ɑ], in the bottom half of the spectrum; the back vowels [o] and [u], at increasingly lower levels. Figure 4.2 also demonstrates that the first formant and the singer's formant are usually prominent in a well-trained voice regardless of vowel or pitch. The presence of these formants ensures resonance balancing in the singing voice.

Increasingly, the acoustic factors of singing are being subjected to investigative study. It is now well established that a sound that strikes the listening ear as aesthetically pleasing (in "classical" singing) is the result of verifiable acoustic and physiologic conditions. Precisely, it is the relationships, adjusted for vowel definition, among the fundamental frequency and the first, second, and third (and at times the fourth and fifth) formants that determine the listener's perception of resonance and the singer's proprioceptive response to the sounds he is making. It is the acoustic energy referred to above, exhibited in the 2500–3300 Hz region regardless of the vowel being defined, that sets the resonant singing voice apart from normal speech. This relationship among the levels of acoustic energy (formants) determines the unique beauty of a singing instrument. It explains the traditional "resonance" of the professional singing voice.

Vowel definition and the constant presence of the singer's formant in a well-balanced series of alternating [e] and [ɑ] vowels, sung by a professional *tenore lirico*, is graphically demonstrated in the spectral analysis of Figure 4.3. A spectrogram, such as the one considered here, displays dis-

FIGURE 4.3. Vowel definition [e] and [ɑ] indicated by spectral analysis of the tenor voice.

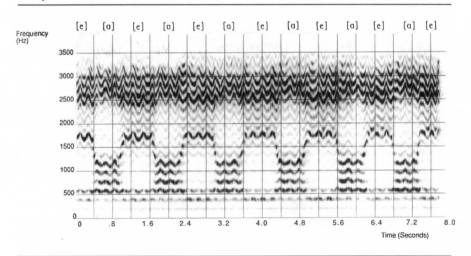

tribution of acoustic energy in a specific time and frequency range. The horizontal axis represents *time,* 0 to 8 seconds in this case. The vertical axis represents *frequency,* 0 to 4000 Hz. The third variable is *acoustic energy,* represented by degrees of darkness observable in different regions of the graph: the darker the region, the higher the concentration of energy.

The regularity of the vibrato rate (the undulations) and the consistency of the singer's formant are shown in Figure 4.3. The exact location of the singer's formant depends in part upon the category of tenor voice. A sturdy tenor instrument may exhibit such activity at slightly lower frequencies than a lighter tenor voice. A lyric tenor voice of good size, or a *lirico spinto,* shows concentrated acoustic energy in the region of 2500–3300 Hz. A young tenor voice that has not yet achieved desirable resonance compactness (the appropriate balance among energy levels within the spectrum) may display unwanted energy concentration as far as 4500 Hz, even when singing in speech-inflection range.

Figure 4.4 shows the results of a quantitative analysis of tones sung by a professional *tenore lirico.* In the trained singer, the singer's formant stays constant through the entire vocal range. The spectral bandwidth remains within a 10 percent variance, even in range extremes.

The sonagram of Figure 4.5 illustrates spectral analysis of phonations by a trained (a) and an untrained (b) tenor. In the trained tenor (a *tenore lirico*) the singer's formant is evident in the region of 2500–3300 Hz. The untrained tenor shows no concentration of acoustic energy in the area of the singer's formant (except for the formant associated with the front vowel [e]), and his phonation records partials as high as 4000 Hz, which are perceived as undesirable noise when singing in speech-inflection range. The trained tenor does not register partials above the 3300 Hz region, having greater compactness of energy within the spectrum.

In addition to the resonance balance achieved through the relationships of first formant, middle formant, and singer's formant to the fundamental frequency, a second factor of resonance unification lies in the phenomenon of *vibrato.* The sonagram of Figure 4.5 indicates a vibrato of approximately 6.0 cycles per second in the trained *tenore lirico,* whereas the untrained tenor voice indicates a straight or uneven pattern. (The vibrato is indicated by the wavy lines of the sonagram.)

The trained singer shows an ability to adjust his vocal tract so as to produce *l'impostazione della voce* (also *imposto*), *Sitz, place, placement* (Italian, German, French, and English equivalent terms) independently of vowel formation. The untrained singer tends to show chiefly the adjustments involved in vowel differentiation.

A comparison of spectrograms of a trained and an untrained tenor on the vowel [ɑ] at the pitch A_3 (220 Hz, notated as A–440 Hz in the treble clef) further illustrates these differences (see Figure 4.6). Clearly, the recognizable resonance phenomena in the skillful singing voice depend on the energy distribution among the upper partials associated with the 2500–3300 Hz factor and are not solely dependent upon the formants of the

FIGURE 4.4. Results derived from measurement of the spectra of tones sung by a professional *tenore lirico*. The top box shows the constancy of the singer's formant over three and one-half octaves. Note the small amount of variability in the middle two-octave range (the normal performance range). The middle box shows the resonance balance expressed in decibels. The bottom box indicates the bandwidth at 15 dB below the determined amplitude of the singer's formant. The bandwidth stays remarkably constant throughout the normal two-octave performance range.

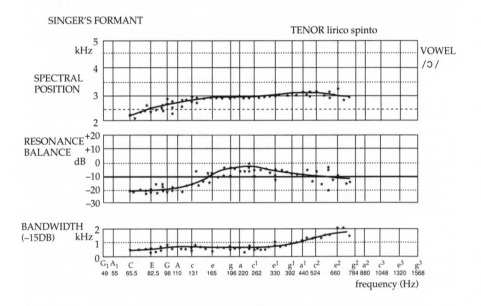

spoken vowels. Despite the fact that the vowel [ɑ] does not have strong partials in the speaking voice in the region of 3000 Hz, the well-trained singing voice shows the same strong band of energy in that region as would be demonstrated by a phonation from the front-vowel series. This, of course, is the singer's formant that assures carrying power and proper resonance balance regardless of vowel.

In the well-trained tenor voice the singer's formant remains constant and must be stable regardless of register transitions or changes. However, "resonance" in the tenor voice cannot be separated from registration timbres. The relationship between resonance balance and registration timbres identified in the historic Italian school (and referred to throughout this work) can become visualized through spectrum analysis. They are

FIGURE 4.5. Sonagram of a tone with vowel change from [e] to [ɑ], sung by a professional tenor (left side, a). The dark band in the spectrum at about 2700 Hz indicates the presence of the singer's formant, regardless of vowel change. Sonagram of the same tone with the same vowel change sung by an amateur tenor (right side, b). (Note the lack of the singer's formant.)

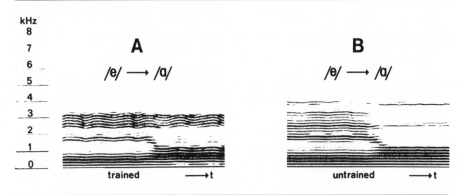

1. *voce di petto* (chest voice)
2. *voce mista* (mixed voice)
3. *voce finta* (feigned voice)
4. *voce di testa*, also termed *voce piena in testa* (head voice)
5. *falsetto* (the imitative sound of the female produced by the male)

These phonations, illustrated in Figure 4.7, were sung at F_4. Timbre differentiations were clearly discernible to the *tenore lirico* who sang them

FIGURE 4.6. Acoustic analysis of the vowel [ɑ] (220 Hz) graphed at moderate intensity (90 dB) sung by a professional tenor (left side, a) and by an amateur tenor (right side, b).

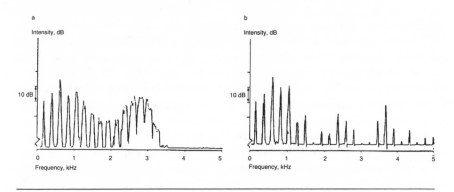

FIGURE 4.7.   Several categories of vocal registers represented in spectral analysis of tones sung by a professional tenor. (In the falsetto portion (e) the fundamental has not been registered.)

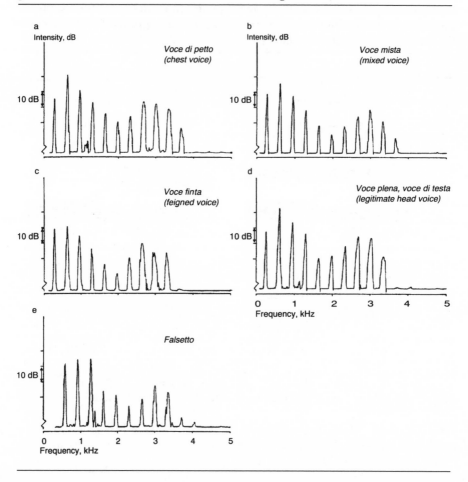

and to the perception evaluators who heard them. As could be anticipated, the greatest differences were found between *voce di petto* and *falsetto* timbres (see Figures 4.7a and 4.7e).

In order to produce F_4 completely in *voce di petto* (it should be kept in mind that F_4 is written for the tenor voice at the upper ledger line [F_5] of the treble clef), the singer experienced extensive muscular tension in the region of the larynx and in the neck and chest, similar to that found in heavy, loud shouting. However, despite the forced character of the production, the phonation still registered the "ring" associated with the singer's formant. This is an important observation, because it proves that tenors (particularly the *robusto* and *Helden*) are capable of producing "ringing" sounds even with "pushed" production. But the price in local effort is high, and a question of vocal efficiency is raised. Pure "chest voice" should never be carried beyond the *primo passaggio* (roughly $C_4^\#$–D_4). As a general rule "chest" should be mixed with "head" even earlier than the *primo passaggio* registration pivotal point. Most well-trained tenors have the subjective feeling that they achieve registration unity over the complete range of the voice by bringing "head voice" sensations downward through an entire descending scale.

Compared with *voce di petto,* the other registration timbres, *voce mista, voce finta, voce di testa* (*voce piena in testa*), are perceived by the singer as much lighter in mechanical action. Their production is more efficient than that of the *voce di petto* phonation at a high pitch such as F_4, inasmuch as they achieve the best result for the least expenditure of effort. (Figure 4.7 indicates the F_4 pitch, where *voce di petto* should not be utilized. However, "chest" *is* appropriate to the greater vocalis-muscle activity undertaken by vocal-fold vibratory function in lower pitches of the *voce di petto* range.)

In the historic international school (based on the Italian vocal practices that predominated in "classical" singing for several centuries), the tenor aims to produce an even scale throughout his range and to minimize changes in vocal timbre, regardless of register. Figure 4.7 shows that these old empirical assumptions were actually based on acoustic phenomena that are currently measurable.

One can logically conclude that the four lighter registration productions (*voce mista, voce finta, voce piena in testa,* and falsetto) result from a lessening of the heavier vocalis action associated with *voce di petto.* (A graduated dynamic muscle relationship, as earlier described, permits constant balancing of the resonance factor in all ranges so that uniformity of timbre is achieved.) These muscular adjustments (all below the level of consciousness, and none of which are locally controllable) are brought about by

1. Isometric contraction of the vocal bands (which changes the quantity of the vibrating mass and the degree of vocal band stiffness)
2. Longitudinal tension of the vocal folds (largely in response to action of the cricothyroid muscles)
3. Medial compression of the vocal folds (chiefly in response to action of the lateral cricothyroid muscles)
4. Laryngeal positioning (effect of the external frame musculature and the laryngeal elevator and laryngeal depressor muscles)

These adjustments occur in cooperation with corresponding breath management activities that determine subglottic pressure and airflow rate. (For more information, consult "Resonance Balance in Register Categories of the Singing Voice; A Spectral Analysis Study," by H. Schutte and R. Miller, 1984, *Folia Phoniatrica 36*, 289–295.)

Voce finta is a timbre that, within a limited range, can easily be turned into *voce mista* or *voce di testa*. One might, therefore, argue that *voce finta* has more to do with dynamic level and energy factors than with actual registration events. As shown in Figure 4.7c, the spectrum analysis of the *voce finta* phonation is not remarkably different from the *voce di testa* (Figure 4.7b), but differences do exist. Falsetto on the other hand (Figure 4.7e) displays marked differences.

Voce di testa and *voce mista* involve similar sensations of physical co-ordination and resonance. As noted earlier, the legitimate head voice (*voce piena in testa*) characterizes the production of the skilled tenor voice in upper range, and the physiologically related *voce mista* occurs chiefly in middle voice (*voce media*), within the *zona di passaggio*. However, *voce mista* can also be carried below the *primo passaggio* into lower middle voice.

Other brief phonations sung by a professional *tenore lirico* (see Figure 4.8) display both changing vowel formants and the constantly present singer's formant. A vibrato rate of approximately 6.0 cycles per second is also indicated.

Based on information thus far considered, it is clear that "resonance" in the singing voice, including all categories of tenor, is dependent on cooperation between resonators above the larynx (supraglottal), action within the larynx as it generates sound, and the value of the airflow. Vocal tract tuning includes vowel tracking (when the right buccopharyn-geal cavity shapes correspond to the laryngeal configurations that initiate vowel production) and formant balancing (the joining of strong harmonics generated by the fundamental frequency with the acoustic energy carried by the formant frequencies). The formant frequencies then naturally line up with the overtones of the source. Such vocal tract tuning is coupled to coordinated breath management. Graduated vocal registration, through the process of resonance balancing and adjusted subglottic pressure and airflow, permits vocal tract tuning throughout the scale.

EXERCISES IN RESONANCE BALANCING

The key to register unification is found in the *zona di passaggio*. What occurs in this region determines register unification and resonance balancing in the great C_3 to C_5 scale (and even for the few publicly performable pitches that may extend on either side). Because of the acoustic nature of the front

FIGURE 4.8. A series of ten vowels, in sequence from front to back, indicates changing vowel formants (vowel definition), the constant presence of the singer's formant (2500 Hz-3300 Hz), as well as degrees of acoustic strength in the lower regions of the spectra. (Pitch B_3.)

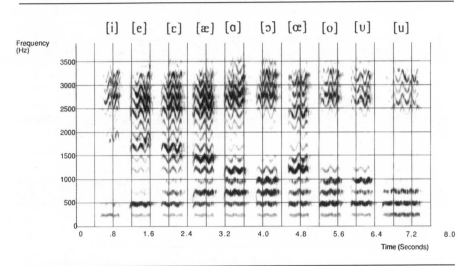

vowels [i] and [e], with peaks of energy concentrated in the region of the singer's formant, those vowels are useful for improving overall resonance balancing in tenor voices. Several famed Cotogni students report that he recommended the set of vowel and pitch sequences of Exercise 4.1 for achieving balanced resonance in all vocal registers: "Con quest'esercizio si fa la voce!" (With this exercise, you build your voice!)

Assuming a D_4 *primo passaggio* register pivotal point, Exercise 4.1 begins in the key of G and proceeds upward by half tones through the key of D^b, then downward by half tones. The reverse vowel order then is sung, so that the vowels are sequentially changed on the fifth note of the scale, with the new vowel remaining during the subsequent descent to the prime (where the vowels again change).

When vowel modification was considered in Chapter 3, examples were given of vocalises and literature passages in which front vowels (especially [i] and [e]) prefaced climactic high-lying phrases or notes. Vowel color and resonance factors are considered by knowledgeable composers when writing phrases that mount to the upper range. Many indications of that awareness are illustrated in the music examples of this study.

The same principle of using a front vowel, which is by its nature high on upper partials in the same region of the spectrum as the singer's formant, can be adopted as a good pedagogical device by its momentary

EXERCISE 4.1

insertion as a pilot sound when the tenor is working on spots in the literature that are difficult for him, particularly those that begin with less-favorable vowels or consonants.

In the same pedagogic direction, a helpful method of initiating tenorial brilliance, especially in the back vowels, is the "bad" vowel. The phoneme [æ] is termed the *bad vowel* because it is found in the word "bad." It is also a vowel often avoided in performance circumstances because of its blatant character. For example, if a tenor were asked to sing the phrase "That bad cat is fat," he would tend to modify the vowel away from [æ] toward the vowel [a], or even to [ɑ], depending on the pitch. The vowel [æ] has a unique spectral envelope, with the three energy peaks (formants) evenly distributed across the spectrum at about 1000 Hz, 2000 Hz, and 3000 Hz, which ensures a strong acoustic energy concentration in the mid-region and upper regions of the spectrum (see Figure 4.9). It is this combination of harmonics that can be used pedagogically to induce the "ring" into subsequently sung vowels. When vowels of the back series [ɑ], [ɔ], [o], [U] and [u] tend to lose "frontal brilliance," a better balance can be established by prefacing "low" vowels with the pilot phoneme [æ] (see Exercise 4.2). The exercise should also be transposed into several neighboring keys.

Of considerable importance in pedagogic practice is the position of the mouth during the formation of [æ] in its role as the last vowel of the front-vowel series. Being both lateral and perpendicular in mouth formation, [æ] induces the acoustic factors of a front vowel while retaining a mouth posture not far removed from the first vowel of the back-vowel

FIGURE 4.9. Spectral envelope for the spoken vowel [æ], as in the word "had."

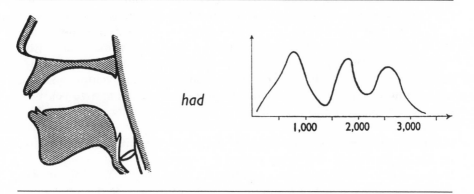

had

1,000   2,000   3,000

Peter Ladefoged, *Elements of Acoustic Phonetics*, tenth impression. Chicago: University of Chicago Press, 1974. By permission.

EXERCISE 4.2

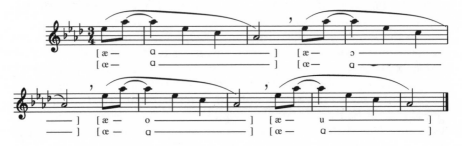

series [ɑ]. For this reason, [æ] often serves well as an intermediary phonetic vehicle for balancing resonance between front and back vowels. The dark/ light (*chiaroscuro*) timbre of the historic international school is often achieved with the aid of the transition vowel [æ]. The phoneme [œ] is similarly useful. (*Chiaroscuro* is a combination of two words: *chiaro* [clear] and *oscuro* [dark], a fitting description of the well-balanced vocal tone. As shown above, the resonance balance of the *chiaroscuro* tone is verifiable through contemporary acoustic analysis.)

The pedagogic virtues of the phoneme [æ] having been extolled, a cautionary word is in order. Exercises such as Exercise 4.2 that are built upon a progression of the phoneme [æ] to a back vowel should not be practiced by any tenor who has a tendency toward "open" sound above the *secondo passaggio*.

The presence of the "ring" (singer's formant) is guaranteed by keeping the same timbre concept in both front and back vowels. This feeling, often termed "forward placement" by singers, may be assisted by using the four nasal consonants (sometimes called nasal continuants because they have pitch duration).

Proprioceptive awareness varies considerably from one nasal consonant to another. A clever singer soon begins to recognize which consonant is most helpful in achieving favorable resonance balance. In general, the nasal [m] directs sensation to the lips; [n], to the zygomatic area (the "upper jaw"); [ɲ], to a more central position at the hard palate; and [ŋ], more centrally in the head. The sudden raising of the velum, and the descending of the tongue in the quick transition from [ŋ] to a vowel, produces favorable conditions in the buccopharyngeal cavity for proper balancing of resonance.

It is helpful for the tenor to locate the precise sensation of each of the nasals, beginning at the *primo passaggio* pivotal note (see Exercise 4.3). Exercises 4.3a and 4.3b use an eighth-note hum on [m] and [n], respectively, with a sequence of changing vowels. Exercise 4.3c does the same thing with the [ɲ] hum, as in the initial sound of the Italian word "gnocchi," the beginning of the second syllable in the English word "union," or the first phoneme of the second syllable of the French word "oignon."

Exercise 4.3d introduces the nasal continuant [ŋ] as found in the concluding phoneme of the word "sung."

EXERCISE 4.3

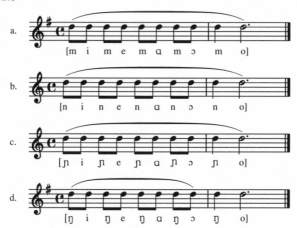

Nasal continuants may be used successfully to preface any exercise pattern dealing with other areas of technical development. Of particular value for a tenor voice are the [ɲ] and the [ŋ] phonemes, which develop sensations of sympathetic vibration in the central areas of the head. Patterns that begin in middle voice, descending and ascending through the *zona di passaggio*, are recommended (see Exercises 4.4 and 4.5).

EXERCISE 4.4

EXERCISE 4.5

Teachers making use of the nasal continuants must always be on guard that the nasal timbre these consonants induce is not carried over into the subsequent vowel. The pure vowel must emerge immediately following the termination of the nasal phoneme. Closing off the nostrils while singing vowels is a very good way to check that no nasality has continued into non-nasal phonation. It is also an excellent device for securing proper velar elevation for all vowel production.

Chapter 5

Developing Agility in the Tenor Voice

The *tenore di grazia* is today identified with the term *bel canto* because his performance literature is in the style of vocal writing epitomized by Bellini, Donizetti, Rossini, and other composers of the first half of the nineteenth century. The designation of the vocal style of that period as *bel canto* is an after-the-fact usage, the current meaning having been applied retrospectively around the 1860s when the newer vocal writing began to demand more dramatic vocalism. Much of the writing for tenor voice prior to the middle of the last century was of a florid nature.

The tenor who sings, for example, the role of Almaviva, *Il Barbiere di Siviglia,* must possess agility in high degree (see Example 5.1). Articulation of rapid passages should not change the timbre of the voice; vocal timbre must not be at the mercy of fast or slow singing. There is an unfortunate current style of singing melismatic passages of the *bel canto* literature by interpolating aspirations (the "HA-ha-ha-ha-HA!" school of articulation), often with slurred pitches occurring on each strong beat.

EXAMPLE 5.1. From "Ecco ridente," *Il Barbiere di Siviglia*, Rossini.

Reprinted by permission of G. Schirmer, Inc. International copyright secured.

It is clear that the *tenore di grazia (tenore leggiero)* requires facility in negotiating rapid running passages. Not so widely recognized is the need for agility from *all* categories of tenors who sing roles from the romantic and even *verismo* literatures of the latter half of the nineteenth century and early decades of the twentieth century. Passages such as Rodolfo's opening lines from the first act of *La Bohème* must be agile, supple, and flexible (see Example 5.2).

The ability to be flexible is a requirement not only of running-note passages, however. Unless a tenor of any vocal weight or category can move his instrument with ease, he will lack freedom in singing *sostenuto*. Mounting tension during soaring, sustained phrases results from static as opposed to dynamic muscle balance. Rigidly fixed abdominal settings produce accumulated fatigue, as does pharyngeal setting. Only *dynamic muscle equilibrium* in the breathing and phonating mechanisms can ensure the freedom necessary for the long vocal lines of Verdi, Puccini, Brahms, and Strauss. The musculature of the thorax and the torso must be in athletic condition to provide the structural support for the aerodynamic/myoelastic singing instrument. Part of the training for professional performance consists of learning how to keep a strong musculature supple, whether one is singing melismatic or sustained phrases.

Agility and suppleness can best be acquired in the singing voice through systematic practice of the *appoggio* technique. The same kind of precision that brings about exact coordination between laryngeal and respiratory muscles in the onset and in sustained singing can be achieved in velocity studies.

AGILITY EXERCISES

Keeping in mind the "noble" posture that is essential to coordinating muscles of the thorax and abdomen, and insisting upon the silent breath renewal that is the hallmark of the *appoggio* system, the singer should begin working on agility through quiet laughter-like maneuvers on an articulated hum, as in *"Hm,* hm, hm, hm, *Hm!"* at a fast tempo. Because his mouth is closed, the singer's awareness of abdominal activity that takes place in the articulation process is heightened. The humming portion of the exercise is followed by legato *gruppetti* on the syllable "ha." (see Exercise 5.1).

EXERCISE 5.1

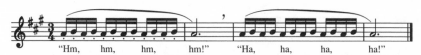

"Hm,   hm,   hm,   hm!"   "Ha,   ha,   ha,   ha!"

EXAMPLE 5.2. From "Nei cieli bigi," *La Bohème*, Puccini.

Reprinted by permission of G. Schirmer, Inc. International copyright secured.

EXAMPLE 5.2.   Continued.

Reprinted by permission of G. Schirmer, Inc. International copyright secured.

The singer retains an easy feeling of "openness" in the anterolateral abdomen (front and sides) and in the rib cage. The quiet, laughter-like articulatory actions are small, gentle impulses; the abdominal wall does not move progressively inward, but almost imperceptibly "bounces" as in quiet, subdued laughter, or as in silent rapid panting.

Exercise 5.2 proceeds from the hum to an open mouth posture on any vowel. The purpose of the exercise is to retain the small supple abdominal action whether on the hum or on the vowel.

EXERCISE 5.2

Following these initial patterns on the hum and on quiet laughter, the same figure should be executed on an articulated legato, with reduced abdominal wall motion but with a continuing sense of suppleness. A useful pattern for maintaining the same posture (that is, remaining longer in the inspiratory position), whether singing a rapid passage or a sustained phrase, is illustrated by Exercise 5.3. The agility exercises should be executed in various keys.

EXERCISE 5.3

Exercise 5.3 is in four consecutive phrases:

1. Articulated hum (like rapid laughter, with the mouth closed)
2. Staccato vowel at fast tempo
3. Legato vowel at fast tempo, but with the same kind of articulatory movement in the epigastric-umbilical region
4. Legato at a slow tempo, with considerably reduced articulatory motion, while remaining in the inspiratory position

In this exercise there should be no inward movement of the front abdominal wall except for miniscule, barely discernible articulatory bounces. One remains flexible in the fast-moving portions of the exercise and then sustains the inspiratory position during the slower portion, avoiding all tension. Breath renewal, as always, must be silent and unforced. Helpful patterns for developing a reliable technique of vocal velocity are found in the group of exercises beginning with Exercise 5.4 and extending through Exercise 5.15. Use any vowel or sequence of vowels.

EXERCISE 5.4

EXERCISE 5.5

EXERCISE 5.6

EXERCISE 5.7

EXERCISE 5.8

EXERCISE 5.9

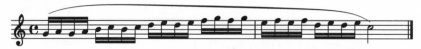

EXERCISE 5.10

EXERCISE 5.11

EXERCISE 5.12

EXERCISE 5.13

EXERCISE 5.14

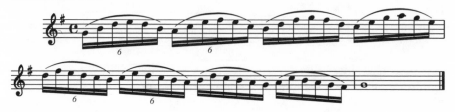

EXERCISE 5.15

It is also useful to combine agility and sostenuto factors within the same exercise so that the flexibility initiated with the agile portion of the exercise is not lost when sustained phonation begins. The articulatory impulses do not continue during the sostenuto, but the sense of looseness remains (see Exercises 5.16 and 5.17).

EXERCISE 5.16

EXERCISE 5.17

The sostenuto portion of these patterns should be lengthened. By combining agility and sustaining factors in a series of exercises, the singer systematically deals with the two poles of *bel canto* literature, *fioritura* and *cantilena.* In many of the great arias from nineteenth-century operas, the singer was expected to display both facets of his art: the *scena* was in *cavatina/cabaletta* (*cantabile/bravura*) form. He presented the long, flowing lines of the *cavatina,* which were followed by the melismatic passages of the *cabaletta.* In preparation for such vocal tasks, numerous velocity exercises were combined with exercises in sostenuto. The literature promoted both factors, frequently even through rapid and extensive embellishment of sostenuto passages themselves, especially in the *da capo.* Exercise 5.18 is an example of the kind of vocalise every category of tenor should practice as an aid in combining agility and sostenuto skills.

EXERCISE 5.18

Such technical drills prepare the tenor for both agility and sostenuto requirements, which are often present within the same aria, as for example in "Il mio tesoro," *Don Giovanni* (see Example 5.3). Short passages should

EXAMPLE 5.3a. From "Il mio tesoro," *Don Giovanni*, Mozart.

be isolated as vocalises, with the gradual addition of longer passages. Aspirated articulation and slurring must be guarded against. An excellent vocalise pattern that may be transposed into neighboring keys (both up and down) is the famous "nunzio vogl'io tornar!" passage, a perfect example of articulated legato (see Example 5.3b).

Some of the same melismatic tasks are present in another well-known tenor aria, "Ev'ry Valley," *Messiah* (see Example 5.4a). Moderately sustained phrases are juxtaposed with velocity passages, illustrating both aspects (*cantabile/bravura*) of Baroque operatic writing for tenor voice. The melismas in Example 5.4b are among the most useful exercises available for accomplishing both agility and a well-modulated scale throughout middle voice. As is almost always the case, Handel is here an excellent teacher of singing! This is also eminently clear in Example 5.4c, in which the *voce media* excursion on "and the rough places plain," and the vocalise occurring twice on "the crooked straight," play with *primo* and *secondo passaggi*

EXAMPLE 5.3b. From "Il mio tesoro," *Don Giovanni*, Mozart.

Operatic Anthology, Vol. III. Reprinted by permission of G. Schirmer, Inc. International copyright secured.

EXAMPLE 5.3b. Continued.

Operatic Anthology, Vol. III. Reprinted by permission of G. Schirmer, Inc. International copyright secured.

and are followed by alternating sostenuto and agility in the long melisma on the word "plain."

Another remarkable, yet typical, Handelian segment that demonstrates melismatic writing in smooth transition through the *zona di passaggio* comes from "Let the Deep Bowl," *Belshazzar*. Obviously vocal display is here as important as textual exuberance. Handel masterfully treats both elements (see Example 5.5). The phrase that begins " 'tis gen'rous wine," playing as it does on the arpeggio in G major, is itself a worthy vocalise. However, the subsequent "exalts," with its descending and ascending patterns in the G_3–G_4 octave is the type of agility exercise every tenor can profitably use in the daily warm-up routine.

Innumerable other examples of the agility factor may be taken from the tenor vocal literature. As fine a pattern as could possibly be devised comes from the first-act Almaviva/Figaro duet from *Il Barbiere di Siviglia* (see Example 5.6). It can be transposed into convenient keys at levels easy to

EXAMPLE 5.4a.   From "Ev'ry Valley," *Messiah*, Handel.

Reprinted by permission of G. Schirmer, Inc. International copyright secured.

execute, then sung in the original key and in several neighboring higher tonalities.

Another valuable example comes from the first-act aria, "Ecco ridente," in the same Rossini opera. The melismas are to be accomplished at whatever tempo permits clean articulation without inserted aspirations. Gradually increase the tempo as facility advances (see Example 5.7).

A third example from the same Rossini source occurs again in the first-act duet between Almaviva and Figaro. Each phrase should be practiced separately as a vocalise, on a single vowel (front and back), and then on the vowels inherent in the text. The final technical work is to return to the original text, linking the phrases together (see Example 5.8).

It is assumed that a singer interested in systematically developing a reliable technique will practice all aspects of vocalism, devoting part of the daily session to representative exercises from each technical area. It would be nonproductive, for example, to do only agility exercises for one complete practice session. Velocity vocalises and similar passages from the literature should be alternated with sustained exercises.

EXAMPLE 5.4a. Continued.

Reprinted by permission of G. Schirmer, Inc. International copyright secured.

EXAMPLE 5.4b. From "Ev'ry Valley," *Messiah*, Handel.

EXAMPLE 5.4b. Continued.

EXAMPLE 5.4c. From "Ev'ry Valley," *Messiah*, Handel.

EXAMPLE 5.4c. Continued.

straight, the crook - ed straight, and rough plac-es   plain, _____

_____ and the rough plac-es   plain.

Reprinted by permission of G. Schirmer, Inc. International copyright secured.

EXAMPLE 5.5. From "Let the Deep Bowl," *Belshazzar*, Handel.

'tis gen-'rous wine, 'tis gen-'rous wine, Ex-

- alts the hu-man to di-vine, ex-alts, ...

By permission Boosey & Hawkes.

EXAMPLE 5.6. From Act I Duet, *Il Barbiere di Siviglia*, Rossini.

C.
la_____ fiam - ma_ sen - - to,
charms_____ and_____ de - lights_____ me!

F.
gen - to, già viene l'o - ro, ec-co-lo qua, già vie-ne l'o - ro, già vie-ne
lights me; Sweet is the mu - sic of my re-ward, Mon-ey con-soles me, Mon-ey al -

cresc.

Reprinted by permission of G. Schirmer, Inc. International copyright secured.

EXAMPLE 5.7. From "Ecco ridente," *Il Barbiere di Siviglia*, Rossini.

EXAMPLE 5.8. From Act I Duet, *Il Barbiere di Siviglia*, Rossini.

EXAMPLE 5.8. Continued.

Reprinted by permission of G. Schirmer, Inc. International copyright secured.

Chapter 6

Learning to Maintain the High *Tessitura*

A look at the *tessitura* of roles sung by protagonists in most operas reveals why the life of the tenor is not always easy. When one considers where the pivotal points of the registers occur in lower male voices and compares them with register demarcation points in tenor voices—and how the relative literatures lie with regard to those register events—one realizes that the tenor has to negotiate a greater number of phrases and sustained notes in upper range than does the baritone or bass with his voice. It may be asked, "Well, why not? Isn't that the expectation for a 'high' voice?" It is no easier for the tenor to sing in the upper third of his voice than for the baritone to do so in his, yet the literature demands it more frequently of the tenor than of any other vocal type. As a result, the breath energy level to be maintained is frequently much higher for tenor voices than is the case for other singers. Register factors in the soprano voice, for example, do not parallel those of the tenor, except for some incidental parallelism of the $F^{\sharp}$–G *passaggio* phenomenon.

It is interesting to examine a standard opera score—such as Puccini's *La Bohème*—and to observe how many of the notes for Rodolfo lie above the *secondo passaggio* pivotal point $F^{\sharp}_4$–G_4, and how relatively few of Marcello's notes lie above his *secondo passaggio*, which occurs at $E^{\flat}_4$. There is little doubt that the role of Rodolfo is far more demanding as regards high *tessitura* than the role of Marcello.

It is not true that the tenor makes use of a special "head-voice extension" not available to other male voices. In elite vocalism the unified scale is achieved in all male vocal categories through the same techniques of resonance balancing with regard to pivotal registration points. The baritone relies no more upon "chest" voice beyond the *primo passaggio* than does the tenor, except in certain pedagogies that advocate forced, pressed phonation. (The expression *"do di petto"* does not, of course, literally mean that the tenor "High C" can be executed in chest voice. The term is sometimes used to describe the *voce completa* character of the legitimate "High C" as opposed to C_5 sung in falsetto production. Even in forced phonation, neither the tenor nor the baritone could carry *petto* into the extremes of upper range without injury to his instrument.)

The role of Mimì is far less difficult as regards *tessitura* than is the role of Rodolfo, even though Mimì may have a comparable number of notes above her $F^{\sharp}_5$–G_5 pivotal point, because she does not require the level of subglottic energy that Rodolfo needs for his $F^{\sharp}_4$–G_4 passage point. (Rodolfo's actual frequency is an octave lower than is Mimì's because any male singing the written pitch 440 Hz [A–440] is, of course, producing 220 cycles per second [cps].) Considering the larger size of his instrument (his laryngeal structure, the character of the surrounding musculature, and other contributing factors of the male physique), his feat in producing a ringing high $B_4^{\natural}$ in the third-act unison duet with the soprano is more remarkable than her $B_5^{\natural}$. Because of physical and acoustic differences between the tenor and soprano instruments, pitches above G_5 do not require the same degree of energization from the lyric soprano that those above G_4 demand of the lyric tenor.

A soprano, for example, should be able to produce at least another third or fourth (often a sixth) in frequencies beyond her C_6 (High C) through development of her flageolet voice. The tenor has no such possibility. (Male falsetto does not equate with female flageolet.) The operatic tenor, with his ringing C_5 (High C) is then producing a pitch that lies close to the extreme of his phonatory range; the soprano clearly is not. Some tenors, however, of a very light category inappropriate to much of the operatic literature, may be able to perform through D_5, and even $E_5^{\natural}$, in quickly moving passages.

A lack of tenor voices, indeed the existence of a so-called crisis in tenors (pointed out in the introduction), is often cited with much tongue clucking by contemporary critics. Yet the same critics seldom mention the exceptional demands faced by the tenor in comparison with other vocal types. One of the reasons there is a shortage of tenors is that it takes great skill to maintain the high *tessitura*, which exceeds that of any other vocal category of comparable size or weight.

Mounting concert pitch levels in the current century (today often even above 440 Hz) in relation to pitch levels of the nineteenth century, from which much of the standard vocal literature stems, more directly affect tenor categories than others. Today's tenor is asked to do dramatic singing at higher pitch levels than were current in the past century. (This is the case with all singers, of course, but it is most telling for the tenor voice, where high *tessitura* is so characteristic of the vocal writing.)

The *tenore di grazia* of the nineteenth century was not expected to make the virile sound later demanded by Verdi, Puccini, and composers contemporary with and subsequent to them. Today, performance expectations even in the so-called *bel canto* literature often call for higher dynamic levels from singers who must perform in large, acoustically unfavorable, barn-like modern opera houses, with enlarged orchestras. This places additional burdens on all tenor categories, but especially on voices of lighter structure.

Because of the responsibility of maintaining the high *tessitura* as well as the romantic nature of most of his roles, the tenor must not only be a vocal athlete but also one who can combine power, virility, grace, bravura, and tenderness. Above all other male singers, the tenor needs to find the proper balance of resonance that produces the complete vocal sound (*voce completa*). In a number of ways he is the most technically exposed of all singers.

Exercises for assisting the tenor, of any category, to develop desirable resonance balance as he enters upper-middle voice have already been suggested in Chapter 4. The following vocalises are useful for maintaining good resonance balance while acquiring vocal skill and stamina for accomplishing the high tessitura so frequently required of him.

EXERCISES FOR THE ESTABLISHMENT OF UPPER RANGE

Exercise 6.1 should be extended through mounting neighboring keys after good resonance balance in *voce media* has been established. A single vowel (probably a front one, initially) is suggested, to be sung at a moderately slow tempo.

EXERCISE 6.1

Of course, it is in the *voce media* that sostenuto must first be stabilized before sustained singing in the upper range of the tenor voice is attempted. Schubert's "Am Meer" (*Schwanengesang*) is an example of a slow, sustained *Lied,* much of which is executed in the *zona di passaggio* (Example 6.1). It is suggested that the tenor first hum individual phrases, then proceed to vowels and finally to the text. Practicing in this fashion on phrases from the literature is an excellent way to find the *chiaroscuro* timbre essential in maintaining this *Lage* (*tessitura*).

The best way to accomplish the high *tessitura* that characterizes operatic literature is to approach it systematically through vocalises that bring about coordination among the breath source, the vibratory source, and the resonator source. Although consideration has already been directed toward entry into the upper range, exercises in maintaining high *tessitura* have been delayed until this point because general freedom in vocal production must first prevail. Exercises 6.2 through 6.7 are technical studies that have proved efficient in developing the upper range associated with much of the tenor vocal literature. The subsequent musical examples can also serve as advanced vocalises.

EXERCISE 6.2

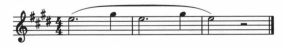

EXAMPLE 6.1.   From "Am Meer," *Schwanengesang*, Schubert.

Used by permission of C. F. Peters Corporation.

EXERCISE 6.3

EXERCISE 6.4

EXERCISE 6.5

EXERCISE 6.6

EXERCISE 6.7

(A continuing assumption is here made that no teacher or singer will expect to accomplish advanced vocalises until those of lesser difficulty have been mastered.)

Another example of a composer writing *voce media tessitura*, although this time at *andante mosso*, may be found in Ernesto's aria, "Com'è gentil," *Don Pasquale* (Example 6.2). The passage serves as an excellent vocalise for combining the factors of breath management, laryngeal freedom, and resonance balancing essential to sustained high *tessitura*. (Note the frequency with which the front vowels are placed at crucial points in the vocal line.)

Similar concentration in the *zona di passaggio* marks the tenor aria "Dai campi" from Boito's *Mefistofele* (Example 6.3). The writing is, of course, heavier than in the Donizetti example and should be reserved for tenors of *spinto* category. In typical Italian-schooled operatic composing, the climactic B$_4^\flat$ occurs on the [e] vowel. The last ten bars provide an excellent exercise in developing the ability to maintain a relatively high *tessitura*.

Flotow, author of eighteen operas but remembered today chiefly for his *Martha* (which is performed in a number of languages), wrote for tenor voice in the international operatic vocal style. The excerpt from the famous tenor aria exemplifies the need for good resonance balance in the *zona di passaggio* and provides tenors with a challenging exercise. Although the aria is often sung by all categories of tenor, it should be reserved for the skilled singer (see Example 6.4).

A fine aria for tenor (best for the *tenore spinto*) is the dramatic "Cielo e mar," *La Gioconda* (Example 6.5). It is an example of demanding, sustained *tessitura*. The excerpt serves as an excellent vocalise, but only for mature, technically secure tenors.

Passages of arias such as "Cielo e mar" should be taken out of context and treated as vocalization segments. The reiteration of the word "vieni" is yet another example of the use of front vowels to introduce phrases in upper middle and upper voice. (The last "vien" is traditionally sung on B$_4^\flat$.)

Librettists, of course, supply the texts to which composers respond. However, there is little doubt that operatic composers of the last century

EXAMPLE 6.2. From "Com'è gentil," *Don Pasquale*, Donizetti.

Operatic Anthology, Vol. III. Reprinted by permission of G. Schirmer. International copyright secured.

EXAMPLE 6.2.   Continued.

Operatic Anthology, Vol. III. Reprinted by permission of G. Schirmer. International copyright secured.

EXAMPLE 6.3. From "Dai campi," *Mefistofele*, Boito.

Opera Songs, Book 3, The John Church Company.

and of the early decades of the twentieth century understood with regard to acoustic factors and vowel modification what tenor vocal instruments could best accomplish.

Perhaps the prime example of vocal writing that takes into account the tenor voice as both an instrument and an emotive vehicle is to be found in "Ingemisco" from the Verdi *Requiem*. The opening nine bars that serve as

EXAMPLE 6.4. From *Martha*, Flotow.

Operatic Anthology, Vol. III. Reprinted by permission of G. Schirmer, Inc. International copyright secured.

recitative offer one of the finest examples of middle-voice (*zona di passaggio, voce media*) writing available to the tenor (see Example 6.6a).

The aria proper, beginning with "Qui Mariam absolvisti," shows Verdi's uncanny ability to juxtapose front and back vowels to the advantage of the tenor voice. Verdi is sometimes accused by modern-day critics of requiring more than singing voices can safely deliver. This aria, by contrast, represents demanding vocal literature written with fullest understanding of the acoustic and physiologic potentials of the tenor voice. The "mihi quoque" passage, mounting through B♭₄, illustrates Verdi's technique of preparing climactic passages for tenor voice with grateful vowel settings (see Example 6.6b).

Richard Strauss, another composer often accused (perhaps with con-

EXAMPLE 6.5. From "Cielo e mar," *La Gioconda*, Ponchielli.

Operatic Anthology, Vol. III. Reprinted by permission of G. Schirmer, Inc. International copyright secured.

EXAMPLE 6.6a. From "Ingemisco," *Requiem*, Verdi.

Used by permission of C. F. Peters Corporation.

siderable justice) of pushing the capabilities of the human voice a step beyond reason, provides the final example of maintaining high-lying *tessitura* for tenor voice. The aria of the Italian Singer is composed in imitation of classical Italianate writing for the tenor instrument. Although this role is one of the briefest in all operatic literature, it is justifiably one of the most prized.

One should note how well Strauss has caught the principle, so closely associated with Italian operatic writing, of favorable vowels set to high pitches. As a result, the *Rosenkavalier* Sänger aria becomes the ultimate study in vowel differentiation and modification in upper range; it serves as an extended exercise in tenorial resonance balancing.

The aria should be attempted only by the most seasoned tenor. It is presented here largely because it represents an ideal of high, sustained vocal writing for the technically secure professional tenor (see Example 6.7).

EXAMPLE 6.6b. From "Ingemisco," *Requiem*, Verdi.

Used by permission of C. F. Peters Corporation.

EXAMPLE 6.7.   From "Di rigori armato il seno," *Der Rosenkavalier*, R. Strauss.

By permission Boosey & Hawkes.

Chapter 7

Assorted Tenor Problems

Seldom is the tenor, or any other singer, unaware of problematic areas of the voice. Too frequently vocal problems are ignored by teacher and singer in the hope they will disappear or diminish with age. Mostly, neither situation happens. It is the premise throughout this book that the voice is a physical and an acoustic instrument, and that when it functions within efficient physiologic and acoustic boundaries the basic sounds of the vocal instrument are conditioned for artistic use, but not until then. Artistry alone does not solve vocal problems. (One does not learn to sing by performing arias with heartfelt emotion!)

A number of problems typical of tenor voices are considered here, and some possible solutions are offered. Systematic pedagogical suggestions described earlier should be recalled when appropriate to a particular problem identified.

"SPREADING" IN THE QUEST FOR "RESONANCE"

In attempting to find "forward production," some tenors confuse excessive brightness with "frontal resonance." The result is an open quality best described as "spread." "Spreading" or "opening" the voice, in the hope of projecting brilliant timbre, makes vowel modification difficult, if not impossible, in the *zona di passaggio* and in upper range. Frequently, tenors who ignore the need for vowel modification tend to sing the top third of the voice too openly. Spreading is not restricted to a particular *Fach*, being found at times among tenors of all categories.

Open timbre comes from using inappropriate postures of the mouth for either vowel or pitch. This practice ignores relationships that properly should exist between the mouth and the pharynx in resonator coupling, and employs a set mouth posture as the means for "opening the throat." Vowel tracking and formant balancing are then significantly hindered. In proper vowel tracking, the resonator tube (buccopharyngeal cavities and other supraglottic areas) changes shape in accordance with the laryngeal configurations demanded by vowels. (See Figure 7.1 for an example of vocal tract shape and corresponding spectra in speech.)

Most often, spreading occurs because the mouth is too widely opened both perpendicularly and laterally. Some less-than-skillful tenors appear to

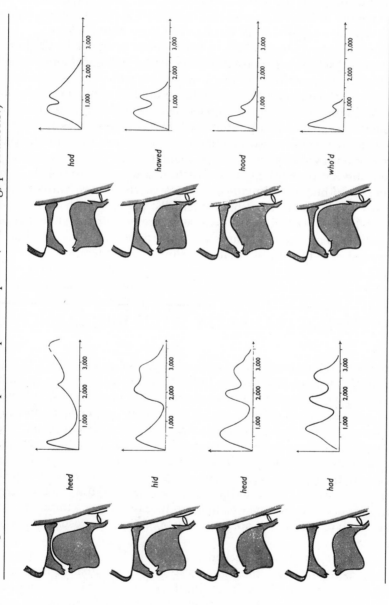

FIGURE 7.1. Changing resonator-tube shapes in changing vowels, with resultant spectral envelopes indicated. (These spectra represent spoken, not sung, phonations.)

heed

hid

head

had

hod

hawed

hood

who'd

Peter Ladefoged, *Elements of Acoustic Phonetics*, tenth impression. Chicago: University of Chicago Press, 1974. By permission.

119

be caught in a permanent gaping "freeze," because they attempt to sing changing vowels by moving only the tongue within one set dropped-jaw posture. (See below, "Sighing, Yawning, and Hanging the Jaw.") This technique is based on the false assumption that vocal timbre can be made uniform throughout the vowel spectrum by maintaining mouth and pharynx in a more or less single posture. The singer is then expected, as much as possible, to sing all vowels through the same mouth shape.

In some schools that adhere to fixed mouth postures for singing, it is the vowel [ɑ] which is supposed to produce the ideal position; in another pedagogical orientation, it is the vowel [i]; in others, it is the rounded vowel [ɔ], or the umlaut [œ], or even [u]. If utilized as the one basic mouth form for singing, each of them impairs vowel differentiation and resonator flexibility. The shapes that produce each of those phonemes are appropriate only to the respective vowels (modified, of course, in mounting pitch), not to some universal posture for phonation.

For the tenor who has been accustomed to using any of these non-efficient fixed-buccal techniques, a series of corrective vowel-definition exercises can be devised on brief intervallic patterns such as 1–3–5–3–1; 5–4–3–2–1; or 1–3–5–8–5–3–1. Vowel sequences of this sort should be sung slowly as the tenor watches himself in a mirror or on a video monitor. The exercises should then be alternated at slow and fast tempos.

CONFUSING NASALITY WITH BRILLIANCE

Formants resulting from the acoustic energy that produces the "ring" in the male singing voice, especially in the tenor voice, generate sympathetic vibrations perceived in the regions of the cheeks (zygomatic arch) and the nasal cavities. Proprioceptive sensations in the "upper jaw" and in the frontal areas of the face have traditionally been described as being "in the masque." They are sympathetic responses of hard body surfaces and bones to supraglottic resonation. Although singers often assume that the frontal sinuses are the chief resonators, the sinuses themselves do not contribute in any major way, if at all, to the actual resonance of the voice. However, when the vocal tract resonances that produce the singer's formant (as well as the depth of the sound) are optimally operative, the resultant sensation is "forward."

Ingo Titze, in an article called "Nasality in Vowels" (1987, *The NATS Journal*), mentions that "there seems to be a perceptual equivalence between nasality and brilliance (ring) in the tone produced." He goes on to say that nasality may produce a perceived increase in brightness of quality, but suggests that the mechanisms for the two types of timbre are different. At the same time, there are similarities in spectral patterns between some forms of nasality and vocal "ring." It may be concluded that although the teacher can use nasal sounds to trick the student into experiencing some sensation in the facial region, he or she should quickly point out that there are preferable ways to obtain those sensations other than through continuing the nasality into the non-nasal sounds.

As described in the chapter on tenorial resonance, one of the best ways to achieve the proper sensation of tone in the head is to occlude the nostrils. Very often a tenor who habitually sings nasally will comment when the nostrils are closed off with the fingers, "But that now *feels* nasal to me!" This is because of vocal tract adjustment that conducts sensations of balanced resonance to the bony and cartilaginous portions of the face, including the nasal cartilages, through sympathetic vibration.

A good way to eliminate nasality in non-nasals is to heighten the singer's awareness of the differences in sound and sensation between the two kinds of timbre. This can be done by having the singer purposely sing a nasal sound, then eliminate it by becoming aware of the difference in feeling between velar elevation and velar lowering. Either the phoneme [k] or the phoneme [ŋ] (both of which induce a lowered velum), followed immediately by a non-nasal vowel (with elevated velum), can bring about excellent results. This is not to suggest that forced velar elevation be introduced but to make it clear to the singer that nasality is caused by a lack of velopharyngeal closure.

As with every tenorial problem identified in this chapter, the singer should have available to him immediate feedback of his recorded phonations so that he may make comparative judgments about the audible differences. Vocal technique ultimately depends on the ability of the singer's own ear to distinguish the differences from one sound to another. The physiologic and acoustic sources that produce these differences must then be identified by teacher and student. The tape recorder can be of much assistance in this process. Further, the ability to *see* as well as to *hear* differences and to associate those differences with *sensation* makes it possible for technical improvement to take place. The video camera is extremely helpful in this process. A further aid lies in the increasing availability of spectral analysis, in which the singer can actually *see* when the harmonic balance is not ideal, the vibrato is uneven, the onset is inexact, the legato is not sufficiently present, or nasality intrudes.

SIGHING, YAWNING, AND HANGING THE JAW

A number of problems that beset the tenor are induced by prevalent and well-meaning pedagogical devices for "relaxing" the singing instrument. It is a mistake easily made by persons who teach but who have not themselves sung professionally. On the surface, insisting on relaxation appears logical. Tension is disastrous to free vocalism. However, the yawn-sigh technique induces slackness in vocal-fold closure, a higher rate of breath emission, and distention of the pharyngeal wall. Vitality and resonance disappear, and the voice is often diminished in size and brilliance.

Most teachers who favor the "yawn-sigh" pedagogy (which was popularized by several prominent voice teachers in the post–World War II period) request that the mandible (jaw) be hung during singing in positions never found in normal phonation nor in life's vital activities. In sighing, one progresses from passing excess breath over the vocal folds to late and incomplete cordal occlusion. Yawning drops the jaw, spreads the pharyngeal wall, and lowers the larynx. It places the velum in a protractedly stretched and tensed position never intended for more than brief duration, a position especially inappropriate to phonation. Yawning, of course, increases the distance between the larynx and the velum, thereby elongating the vocal tract. That might seem like a good thing, but when it is an excessive action it is not. The timbre of the singing voice then becomes distorted and undergoes as much loss of brilliance as does the speaking voice when one yawns. Above all, yawning takes away the vitality of the performance and the excitement of communication. No one has ever experienced a visceral thrill from hearing a sighing/yawning vocal performance. The technique is clearly associated with a group of Germanic/Nordic voice researchers and schools of singing, and does not adhere to resonation principles of the historic international school. (It is based upon speech pathology techniques appropriate to the correction of pressed phonation.)

When the tenor, however, suffers from pressed sung phonation (see "The *Spinto* Complex" below), some favorable changes may be brought about, at least temporarily, by a few moments of vocal exercise built upon the sigh. (Similarly, if the problem is laryngeal elevation, some temporary work with the *incipient* yawn may be useful in discovering a more appropriate lower laryngeal posture.) But because of the high rate of breath emission introduced by the sigh, causing incomplete glottal closure, subsequent onsets are frequently breathy and nonvibrant. (After a badly initiated onset, it is difficult to recover the dynamic muscle balance essential to good phonation.)

The yawn-sigh technique (which peaked in the early 1950s as a major part of vocal pedagogy) is still found among some teachers who believe singing should always feel "relaxed." Such a doctrine is ruinous for tenors. Muscle tonus is essential in all singing but especially for the demands of the tenor literature. Any tenor trying to "open his throat" through yawning, sighing, and dropping the jaw should take another look at the *gola aperta* techniques of the historic schools.

The correction for problems caused by vocal techniques of sighing, yawning, and jaw dropping is simply to give up such nonfunctional approaches to healthy phonation and to establish more efficient and natural pathways of coordination. (Breathy phonation is a pathological condition.)

The best route for eliminating distortion of the vocal tract is to turn to the corrective vowel-differentiation and resonance-balancing exercises presented earlier.

THE PROBLEM OF LARYNGEAL INSTABILITY

"Necktie" tenor is an unkind but appropriately descriptive adjective for the tenor who raises his larynx in inhalation, or at the onset, or with mounting pitch. An elevated larynx is to be avoided in any vocal category, just as certainly as should the forcibly depressed larynx. In proper inhalation, the larynx descends slightly and should remain in that position during singing. There are no exceptions for tenors (except for the occasional *voce finta* coloration).

As noted in the discussion of vocal categories and registration factors, the male speaking voice is related to the "chest" voice of historic vocal pedagogy. Most young males, when singing pitches beyond the speaking range of the voice, tend to thrust the chin forward and to move the head upward. This is because they are unaccustomed to spoken phonation on those pitches except through calling. Laryngeal elevation accompanies these actions.

A tendency to raise head and chin is often related to elevation of the tongue. Indeed, elevating the base of the tongue raises the larynx because the tongue/hyoid bone/larynx mechanism forms an anatomical unit. When the back of the tongue is elevated, the hyoid bone and the cartilaginous housing of the larynx mount. This action shortens the vocal tract (resonator tube), thereby producing thin and distorted timbre.

The three most frequent sources of tension in the singing voice are (1) the tongue, (2) the jaw, and (3) the neck. The tongue occupies much of the vocal tract and is largely responsible (together with the jaw) in effecting the phonetic changes that take place during communicative phonation, whether in speech or in singing. Tenors are not immune from the tongue problems common to all singers. Because it is a universal pedagogical problem not specifically related to tenor voices, a few general suggestions must suffice here.

The body of the tongue on the front vowels must be higher in the front of the mouth while correspondingly lower in the back, and the reverse tongue postures (high back elevation and lower frontal posture) must occur for the back vowels. The apex of the tongue, however, must always rest at the lower front teeth for all vowel formation—where it is when one pronounces an affirmative "Mm-hm!" Tenors in particular often encounter problems when the tongue does any of the following maneuvers:

1. Tongue descends to the roots of the teeth, thereby increasing frontal tongue elevation

2. Tongue is pulled back directly from its home base with the teeth
3. Tip of the tongue is elevated upward in a retroflex posture
4. Tongue is pulled away from points of contact at the sides of the mouth, humping up in the middle
5. Tongue is raised at its sides, held against the upper molars

Patterns of the vocalises designed for vowel differentiation can be borrowed for use as tongue corrective exercises (especially patterns such as 1–3–2–4–3–5–4–2–1, 1–3–5–3–1, and 8–5–3–1), to be prefaced with a consonant that is formed at the acoustic at-rest posture of the tongue, as in the phoneme [v]. Because [v] finds the natural location for the tongue, it serves as a pilot consonant for the subsequent vowel posture. One uses the syllables [vi–ve–vɑ–ve–vi], for example, while observing oneself in the mirror, to ensure that the apex (tip) of the tongue does not move from its initial contact with the teeth established by the consonant [v].

As with tensions of the tongue, jaw problems (mandibular tensions) are common to many singers, not just to tenors. In the previous discussion of vowel definition, vowel modification, and resonance balancing, reference was made to mandible positions during singing. However, some singers tend to be hampered by four distinct jaw problems:

1. The jaw is dropped too far
2. The jaw is not opened sufficiently for the required phonetic postures
3. The jaw is thrust forward
4. The jaw is thrust upward (Problems 3 and 4 are often joined)

Mild, lateral movement of the jaw in small, quick motions during a sustained single pitch, then stopping the jaw action while continuing to sing the tone, often informs the singer where jaw tension lies. Lateral chewing exercises, while humming, are useful as well. Above all, a commitment to the acoustic rules of phonetic production, so dependent on jaw posture, is the best antidote for mandibular tensions.

Neck tensions do not exist for the singer who has mastered the axial orientation of the body that is required for the *appoggio* system of breath management. Exercises for arriving at body alignment, visible as the "noble" position, ensure that the external frame support by the neck musculature is coordinated with the musculature of the torso, to which it is attached. (These exercises are described below in considerable detail.) However, another excellent device for checking on complete freedom of the neck in singing is to very gently shake the head back and forth sideways in very quick, small movements while sustaining a tone, then to stop the motion while continuing the phonation.

Whenever the larynx is maintained at a less than optimal posture in phonation, airflow rate is adversely affected. The stabilized larynx, neither ascending nor descending for pitch change, nor bobbing about in an unsupported way with syllabic definition, is essential to all good singing. Studies with international singers of note prove that laryngeal position remains stable in elite vocalism.

If the external-frame function of the neck (the supportive musculature of the larynx) is kept in dynamic muscle balance, the larynx will remain well-poised throughout the vocal scale. It might be presumed that such an elementary fault as laryngeal elevation would have been eliminated during early years of training, yet a number of potentially successful tenor voices are hampered throughout their careers by problems of the rising larynx.

Several devices may be helpful, if elevating the larynx is a problem. In all of the following corrective suggestions, the singer should observe himself in a full-length mirror. (What we are unaware of we cannot correct.)

1. Being certain that good axial body position has been established (head, neck, and torso in "noble" alignment), with the head positioned at normal eye-contact level, place both hands on the front top of the head, allowing the slight weight of the arms to inhibit any tendency toward head elevation during an ascending scale.

2. Positioning the palms of the hands just below the mastoids (lower region of the head as it joins the neck) and in contact with the mandible (the jaw), maintain that solid posture while practicing mounting triads, arpeggios and scale passages. This device alerts the singer to any tendency to choreograph pitch changes through head postures. The reverse hand posture, with the backs of the hands in the same location, is sometimes less confining and less likely to alter the auditory return perception.

3. Lightly rest the chin in the curve of the forefinger and thumb, with the butt of the hand resting on the chest (or on the other arm positioned across the chest, if the singer is flat chested). Any tendency to move the chin forward or upward with mounting pitch will be noted.

4. Place one hand on the bulbous portion of the back of the head (occipital bone) to check against head elevation while singing a mounting arpeggio or scale. One immediately becomes aware of any motion of head or neck.

5. The use of two mirrors, a hand mirror and a full-length wall mirror, often allows the singer to see whether body alignment (and therefore stable laryngeal position) remains during changes of pitch.

6. The following suggestion should be used only in difficult cases and only when teacher and student are working together. Maintaining the compact axial posture, the singer places the forefinger and middle finger lightly on his neck, just above the thyroid cartilage (above the "Adam's apple") and sings. The attempt is not to restrain the larynx but to see that

it remains in a stabilized position throughout the phonation and with the subsequent renewal of the breath.

Some tenors, usually those with instruments of good size, keep the larynx low with breath intake and during phonation but then allow it to fly upward with the release of the sound. This means that there is too much activity during phonation on the part of the laryngeal depressor muscles, so that pressure must be released in order for the singer to renew the breath. The subsequent breath is noisy, and because the larynx has popped up with the termination of the sound and with the breath renewal, the larynx has to be lowered again for the subsequent onset.

If the breath intake is silent, the larynx will be in optimum stable position for singing. The larynx does not rise with the onset of sound (of course, certain consonants cause small laryngeal movements), and above all, the larynx should not rise at the release of the sound. This is because the release is the new breath; laryngeal elevation at inhalation is a serious technical fault in singing. Posture and breath coordination are the twin pillars of good vocal technique, and they strongly influence laryngeal position. The entire question of problematic laryngeal elevation diminishes as the tenor's ear becomes accustomed to uniformity of timbre and vibrancy in the mounting scale. No singer's larynx should bob up and down with pitch change or breath renewal.

THE "*SPINTO* COMPLEX"

The tenor who is convinced that output of power is the most important form of vocal communication suffers from the "*spinto* complex." With increasing frequency, conductors encourage lyric tenors to sing *spinto* roles and *spinto* tenors to sing *robusto* roles, assignments that are too heavy for them. The vocal-tragedy landscape is littered with tenors whose careers have been terminated early by taking on the roles of Lohengrin or Otello when they should have stayed with Rodolfo.

Unfortunately, today's conductors generally do not emerge from the lyric theater as was once the case, and their knowledge about vocalism is often limited to what they like to hear (which may not necessarily correspond to what is appropriate to the health of the instrument). No voice can be enlarged beyond its natural morphological boundaries, nor is there need to try to do so. When proper resonance balance, good breath management, and the skills of articulation are coordinated, a voice "projects" in a hall, regardless of the size of the voice. If a singer attempts to produce timbre of a weightier character than that suited to his *Fach*, vocal deterioration will occur over a period of time. The sooner he abandons the *spinto* complex, the more likelihood there is that he will recover his vocal health.

A tenor with an instrument of fair size may misunderstand what is meant by the nomenclature *tenore spinto,* believing that he must literally push the sound. The *spinto*'s capability for lyricism must be equal to that of his more *lirico* colleague. Resonance balance cannot be achieved or maintained in the singing voice by excessive vocal-fold occlusion and extreme rates of subglottic pressure. In general, the same relative energy levels should be present regardless of the native weight of the voice. That is, the right degree of airflow and the exactitude of laryngeal action for the demands of pitch, vowel, and volume must be realized through the same efficiency of production in each tenor voice, regardless of category. It is not the case that a *tenore spinto* needs to drive his sound while the *tenore leggiero* relaxes his. Stylistic matters must be taken into account, but efficient vocal production is efficient vocal production for any tenor vocal category.

In attempting to produce more heroic sound than the instrument indigenously possesses, some tenors resort to a high rate of glottal occlusion that resembles the sphincteral action occasioned by heavy-duty lifting or shoving. The singing then becomes marked by unsteadiness of vibrato, pitch problems, and timbre distortions. Musical subtleties become impossible. Finally, vocal health is impaired.

AVOIDING THE "CALL" OF THE VOICE

Another form of driving the instrument can be found in a technique built on the "call" of the voice. In this case the tenor attempts to call when singing pitches that extend beyond normal speech range. Those who advocate this technique believe they are recovering the primitive power of the voice (*die Urkraft der Stimme*). The technique requires heavy vocalis muscle involvement and negates the registration process by which elongation and thinning of the vocal folds occurs in rising pitch.

When the upper-middle voice of the tenor is built on the "call," the higher harmonic partials of the spectrum are not sufficiently prominent; relationships among lower and upper regions of the spectrum are distorted. Such a production is not far removed from yelling in the speaking voice. Although intended to be "heroic," the sound resembles bellowing.

If a tenor is accustomed to producing disconnected breathy sound above the *primo passaggio,* however, an occasional utilization of called speech may be useful in identifying the energy levels necessary for good phonation in the upper-middle voice. However, in an aggressively produced tenor voice, it is wise to avoid any use of imitative calling, even as a momentary pedagogical device.

Humming and exercises that preface vowels with nasal continuants are beneficial in establishing the *chiaroscuro* timbre lacking in heavy vocal production. In the *voce media* where it is often advocated, "calling" in the singing voice produces an imbalance between airflow, subglottic pressure, and vocal-fold approximation.

THE INTERNALIZED TENOR VOICE

At the opposite pole from those voices that tend to "push" or "call" is the internalized tenor who seeks to retain vocal sound within himself. He inhibits vocal tract flexibility through restrictive postures of the mouth, and he exerts pressure on the external muscles of the neck by elevating his head, assuming such posture will increase artistic communication. Straight tone and thin timbre result. Spectral analysis of such singing indicates an imbalance among the three major formants of the singing voice.

Internalized sound is often mistakenly assumed to convey musical and expressive intent. The tenor who savors the internally contained sound does not communicate either vocal sound or interpretation to the outside world. The way the voice sounds inside one's own head does not always match the reality of the emergent sound. A singer has to learn to externalize the sounds that he experiences proprioceptively—to listen on the outside, not on the inside.

Among all categories of singer, vocal sausage makers are legion. They work under the false assumption that every note on the page must be given some kind of dynamic or coloristic change, while overlooking the more important aspects of legato and phrase shaping and phrase direction. Individual notes and syllables then suffer from meaningless crescendo and decrescendo—sausaging—all in the name of sensitive interpretation. The tenor who suffers from the sausage syndrome should be put on a diet of sostenuto vocalises such as those found in Chapter 4. A singer may try to convince himself, his teacher, and the public that the vocal gingerbread with which he decorates his performance stems from artistry when, in fact, it is the product of a shaky technical foundation. Making effects to mask the inability to sing a "supported" legato line is not acceptable in professional vocal circles.

Problems of undersinging or oversinging are almost always related to both physiological and psychological factors. Singers sometimes have tonal concepts that they hold in the hope of sounding interesting, or they have a self-image that inhibits the actual realization of the true vocal instrument. In any event, in the world of the professional tenor, there is no room for either "peepers" or "shouters," no matter what size the instrument. Truthfulness in vocal timbre comes from the body's efficient response to a mental concept of tonal beauty. That concept must engender both artistic imagination and healthy physical answers. Singing that is either mannered and precious, or blustering and aggressive, is neither truthful nor efficient.

SPECIAL PROBLEMS RESULTING FROM FALSETTO TRAINING

(Countertenoring and the special requirements for using falsetto as a viable performance medium are not under consideration here. Please see the brief comments on the countertenor in Chapter 1.)

At the outset of any comment on falsetto usage, terms must be clarified. Despite Garcia (*Mémoire sur la voix humaine*, 1840, p.11), falsetto has never been regarded at large as that part of the range found directly between chest voice and head voice. Garcia's terminology clearly refers to what was universally regarded as *voce media* even in his own time. Physiologic factors of falsetto production, as verified by research, set it apart from the *voce piena in testa* (full voice in head) and from the mixed voice (*voce mista, voce media, voix mixte*) registers. Although the vocal folds are thinned and elongated in falsetto just as in the *voce piena in testa*, laryngeal action that brings about full vocal-fold closure is not, as we have seen, present in falsetto. The intricate balancing of the intrinsic laryngeal muscles that produce the complete head voice does not occur in falsetto production. Therefore, pitches are easier in falsetto than in *voce piena in testa*. For that reason, it might seem that falsetto could be a ready answer to extending the tenor upper range. (Some teachers endorse that view.) Recall, in the international school of elite vocalism, falsetto is reserved for comic effects and for marking (saving energy) during rehearsals. It serves as a marking technique because the skillful coordination of dynamic laryngeal muscle action and breath energy essential to legitimate tenor timbre in the upper range is bypassed. In popular singing idioms, among amateur choristers, in some theories of early music vocal sound, and with countertenors, falsetto has some legitimacy. It has none in the public performance of the professional tenor solo literature.

However, falsetto is pedagogically valuable in mitigating the rigid setting some tenors employ on vocal onsets in upper-middle and upper voice, as was previously noted. Falsetto may also be used pedagogically to good effect in demonstrating acoustic postures of the mouth when one is practicing high-lying passages.

Some of the confusion regarding the mechanics of falsetto production stems from widely disseminated pedagogical literature of the late 1940s and early 1950s, in which the reader was assured that there were only two registers—chest (modal) and falsetto—and that the singer must learn to blend them. This misunderstanding came about because certain researchers themselves lacked sufficient information about professional singing techniques, particularly with regard to the tenor voice, and because they failed to take into account the registration practices of which the professional male singer is capable. In some instances these researchers relied on judgments of singing teachers who had not been professional performers themselves and who applied the language of therapeutic speech research to performance areas that go far beyond speech.

Fortunately, the notion that falsetto can serve as the performance timbre of the upper range in the tenor voice has lost much ground in the last decade. This is partly because falsetto technique has become so patently part of countertenor production and is clearly not the sound of the tenor voice. Unfortunately, a number of tenors have been trained in falsetto methods for accomplishing upper range, and they share the common problem of never having found an acceptable top voice for public performance.

Most tenors who rely on falsetto production for the upper third of their negotiable scale never achieve proper breath management in that range of the voice, because falsetto requires more breath emission than does the more complete vocal-fold approximation of *voce piena in testa*. The tenor who has relied on falsetto in the hope of developing the upper voice almost never achieves a professionally acceptable vocal timbre.

Singing high-lying pitches in falsetto does not, as some advocates of falsetto practice maintain, remove anxiety about singing high notes. Any tenor realizes that the physical events in singing falsetto are very different from those needed for *voce piena in testa*. He regards it as a "hedge" and generally admits reluctance in using it. Such reluctance has nothing to do with assuming a macho role, as some commentators would have us believe, but is due to the tenor's recognition that falsettoing is a form of tenor vocal masquerading.

Constant reliance on the imitative female sound in the male voice (falsetto) may actually cause pathological conditions, just as it does when it becomes a psychologically oriented speech mode in certain clinical cases. In the same way that the constant use of a stage whisper (in which vocal-fold closure is not as efficient as in normal speech) can cause pathological conditions in the speaking voice, so can heavy reliance on falsetto in the singing voice. (It is recognized that countertenors must learn exceptionally good breath management to counteract inefficient airflow factors.)

Sometimes teachers less experienced in dealing with the potentially professional tenor voice expect the "real" tenor to sing pitches in upper range with the same ease with which those frequencies can be negotiated in the female voice. Therefore they assume falsetto is a logical register by which to gain entry into the upper range. In an attempt to avoid tensions common to young tenor voices, they run the risk of permanent physical and psychological damage to the potential tenor by introducing bad habits of unhealthy phonation. Pushing breath over slack vocal folds may be as damaging as pressed phonation.

When a tenor suffers from the detrimental effects of falsetto training, there is nothing to be done but to start over in helping him discover proper vocal registration from the *primo passaggio* upward. Exercises for retraining the falsely classified baritone may be equally helpful, when adjusted for tenor range, in ridding the voice of the pseudo-tenor falsetto sound. It requires great patience from teacher and tenor to recover from the substitution of falsetto for *voce piena in testa*. However, by beginning with the *passaggio* vocalises advocated earlier, *voce completa* can replace the falseness of falsetto as registration practice for the tenor in upper voice.

It should be recalled, however, that there are some pedagogical, as opposed to performance, uses for falsetto. As earlier noted, an onset in falsetto with an immediate transition to *voce mista* or *voce piena in testa* may reduce the tendency toward rigid muscular setting.

THE EARLY DEVELOPER AND THE LATE BLOOMER

A voice teacher seldom faces the problem of tenors who are early developers, yet in the lighter categories occasionally a late teenager will already have an extensive range that coordinates proper registration and resonance factors. In such cases, the teacher's chief duty is to help the young tenor realize the advisability of not singing dramatic literature too soon. Young people who sing well always have a problem in waiting until they are old enough for their voices to be taken seriously professionally. If they can handle a fair amount of the literature of their category, they inevitably want to expand into heavier material. It is the teacher's job to instill patience.

Because the art of singing is somewhat complex (although simple, with regard to basic functional rules), there is quite enough technical work to do even with the relatively secure young singer. Beyond considerations of technique, part of instruction is to provide an appropriate picture of what lies ahead in the professional world. The technically advanced young tenor should be allowed to sing only literature that he can handle without fatigue. His most important lesson to learn: *waiting*.

Finding proper repertory for the young tenor is a task equalled only by the search for suitable repertory for the young bass. Young male singers cannot be expected to sing in as commanding a fashion the same quantity of literature as do their female peers. The reason lies in the effects of puberty, which are considerably more drastic for the male larynx than for the female. A nineteen-year-old soprano has a nineteen-year-old voice. Her male friend of the same age has an instrument only four or five years old. Many male voices, particularly those that change late, remain unsettled well into their mid-twenties.

For the most part, young tenors aged sixteen, seventeen, and eighteen should be forbidden all operatic material, no matter how light in character. It is a common error to think that giving a young tenor a Mozart or Bellini aria is the safe way to proceed. There is not a better way to destroy a young tenor voice. The dynamic subtlety and contrasts required for the so-called *bel canto* literature go far beyond the technical ability of almost any teenage tenor. Certainly, if the beginning singer's voice is heavier than a *tenorino* or *leggiero*, Mozart arias are suicidal. Tenors who have too early begun to sing Mozart, Donizetti, Bellini, and Rossini often develop extreme tensions and phobias (regarding both *tessitura* and individual high notes) that may take years to overcome.

Young tenors at about age eighteen should spend their time working systematically on the kinds of technical skills detailed in this volume. The most difficult problem for those who teach the young is how to inspire them with the discipline it takes to learn a skill such as singing. In an era of instant gratification, and of electronically available information to which one may refer without the need of spending time in mastering it, a major task in teaching the young singer is assisting him (her as well, of course) to be willing to invest the time and patience it takes to learn to sing.

The youthful tenor needs to spend time developing general musical skills and proper language articulation for singing. The importance of the IPA (International Phonetic Alphabet) should be stressed to him. Vocal literature should be restricted to songs in English (if that is his native language), including some of the less-demanding songs and arias of Purcell and Handel, *arie antiche*, nondramatic *Lieder*, and the simpler, range-limited *mélodies*, if he has sufficient language skills.

By the second or third year of professional music-school training, some modest arias should be appropriate. To assemble a list for recommendation to all young tenors is dangerous; the difficulty of any aria varies considerably with the size of the voice that will sing it, the future professional status of that voice, and its current level of technical accomplishment. In general, the greater the professional promise of the tenor, the harder it is to find arias appropriate to early stages of instruction. The urge to sing the aria repertory should be curbed until at least some degree of vocal maturity is in evidence. The teacher is responsible for that decision.

For some tenor voices of college age, the easier Bellini *Canzoni da camera*, some of the Rossini, Verdi, and Donizetti songs (not the arias), and brief, light, florid arias of the early Baroque provide good literature sources. A large body of vocal music from American and British composers is ideal for this age group. A number of admirable song collections exist for young voices.

With the late-blooming tenor voice, the same techniques appropriate to any tenor category apply. Here the main question is, how late is too late? Although there have been notable exceptions, the aspiring tenor past thirty should seriously consider the immense problems entailed in beginning a professional career in singing. Singing is a career in which one must be old enough for the instrument to have reached maturity and technical security but young enough to be convincing on stage. (Unlike a degree in business administration, a degree in voice performance does not mean one may go job hunting.) Very often the tenor who is a vocal late bloomer is also a late bloomer musically, in which case his chances for a professional career are further diminished. It is not solely the vocal endowment that ensures a career but the entire package of beautiful vocal sound, musicianship, artistry, and physical appearance. Some of these qualities are endowments while others require tremendous personal discipline. For the person who has been unable to put his life together in general by the time he reaches thirty, the possibility of achieving great success in a vocal career is small. Learning the discipline of singing is to learn a discipline for living.

Singing just for pleasure is an entirely different matter. No one is too old for that, including late-blooming tenors who study voice for pleasure. But expecting to sing professionally is a risky business at best, and it probably is unrealistic to have professional career goals if one starts quite late from both vocal and musical aspects. However, if a tenor in his mid-twenties has a voice that has been identified by those qualified to judge as a voice of exceptional beauty, and if he has the ability to communicate and shows evidence of innate musicality, he is not foolish to devote himself to professional preparation. In some respects, his progress will be more rapid because he is mature enough to incorporate technique. In any event, common sense dictates that anyone who is a late beginner ought to have other skills and training on which he can rely if a singing career fails to develop. With a safety net beneath him, his singing career aspirations may be more logical.

There is also the late-blooming tenor who finds himself in that category because he was falsely classified as a baritone in the first decade of his adult life. A consideration of his situation follows.

FROM BARITONE TO TENOR

Improper classification of vocal category, particularly among male voices, is common. Singers generally have fine imitative facility and can produce several kinds of acceptable vocal quality simply by mirroring what they assume to be desirable timbre. Often the young male singer tries to produce a big, dark sound that he equates with masculinity. If vocal category is to be accurately determined, the teacher of singing needs to locate those pitches that are not encumbered with manufactured timbre.

Sometimes the wide range of categories within the tenor classification is not recognized, and voices that exhibit registration events appropriate to heavier tenor instruments are perceived as indicating a baritone, or even a bass-baritone. Nor is range an entirely reliable indicator of vocal category, inasmuch as some tenors have a good low G_2 and some baritones do not. A baritone, on the other hand, may actually have a better A_4 than the potential tenor. Many young tenors do not know how to achieve entry into upper voice, and if the voice is sizable they may well be falsely classified as baritones.

Physical structure may be a useful clue. However, body build is not a totally dependable indication of vocal type. It is not always the case that males with large laryngeal prominences are destined to be baritones or basses. Some assistance in determining *Fach* can be found by considering how the speaking voice is used. And yet, the most certain aid in determining voice classification concerns the identification of registration pivotal points, as discussed in Chapter 1.

There are singers who have tried to fit themselves into a baritone mold for a number of years but have never felt comfortable doing so. More than one professionally active baritone has made the decision to interrupt his career in order to make the change to tenor.

There are several signs that indicate a tenor may have been incorrectly classified as a baritone:

1. Upper-middle voice (*zona di passaggio*) may feel heavy and difficult to move.
2. Fatigue sets in quickly.
3. The timbre of pitches near the *secondo passaggio* does not match other areas of the voice.
4. The throat feels it is closing when "cover" is attempted in upper-middle and upper voice.
5. The voice is more flexible when less dramatic sounds are produced.
6. When more vocal freedom prevails, the baritone timbre takes on a tenorial character.
7. Casual vocalization into upper range is much easier than maintaining the middle *tessitura*.
8. Coaches and contest judges who regularly deal with professional male voices always ask, "Are you sure you are not a tenor?"

In the interest of objectivity, however, it must also be said that a majority of the above conditions would have to be met to indicate that a baritone is an undiscovered tenor.

Voices that have been falsely darkened or "enlarged" to fit a predetermined concept of timbre cannot arrive at efficient harmonic balance in the spectrum. A complete timbre (*voce completa*) exhibits harmonic strength in both lower and upper portions of the spectrum (*chiaroscuro* tone). Dark, "woofy" singing results from pharyngeal spreading and from the superimposition of timbre concepts foreign to the instrument. Shaping the resonator tube so as to produce darker sounds, makes it difficult to properly assess category. The mistake begins when teachers assume all tenors should sound "light" and "high." As has been repeatedly pointed out, there are many categories of tenor voice, some of them heavier and more dramatic than some kinds of baritones. It is impossible to track the vowel and balance the formants if tone must be darkened to meet some preconceived concept. Attempts to make an inherently tenor voice more like a baritone upsets the concerted action between airflow, laryngeal action, and resonator filtering.

The test for an instrument that appears to be over-weighted is to say "Um-hm!" a few times as one would in a cheerful affirmation. This tends to locate the comfortable speech range (although it is not here assumed that there is some optimal pitch at which the voice phonates). Next, spoken "Ha!" syllables should follow, at a dynamic level appropriate to stage speech. A vibrant singing tone is then introduced in the spoken syllable at the same pitch level. There should be no marked change in production from the spoken syllables, so that no falsification of the sound occurs when singing commences. The point at which a singer feels the need for some additional energy (more "support," "the lift of the breath") will correspond to the termination of the speaking voice (the *primo passaggio*). This timbre is then extended in short upward and downward patterns (see Exercise 7.1 and Exercise 7.2).

EXERCISE 7.1

EXERCISE 7.2

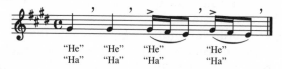

At the *primo passaggio*, exercises that heighten the feeling of "head resonance" become important. Nasal continuants, as noted earlier, often assist that function.

For some weeks or months, most of the work in changing from baritone to tenor should take place in the lower-middle range (not yet in the hoped-for higher register) and in the *zona di passaggio*, as far up as the *secondo passaggio*. Until lyric singing and tenorial timbre have been established in that tessitura, the upper range should be only lightly touched in quickly moving passages. (An exception to this practice is discussed below.) Rapid passages into upper voice should, of course, occur relatively early in the period of category change, so that the ex-baritone can get some idea of the potential range expansion. However, he should not expect to jump immediately into sustained singing in upper voice.

If, while directing most of his attention to the elimination of false "heavy" production, he can sing rapid arpeggios and scale passages into the tenor upper range, that is a positive sign. Patterns of an agile nature can be practiced in series, beginning just below the *primo passaggio*, then mounting above it (see Exercise 7.3). Reminder: most early technical work during the change of category should occur in lower-middle and upper-middle registers until ease and security with the new timbre have been established.

Before moving directly to some typical patterns, a word should be said regarding the baritone-about-to-become-a-tenor who *already* has discovered more ease singing above his *secondo passaggio* than he has in his lower baritone production because he is unable to falsify his timbre in the extreme upper range. In his case, he may be wise to use 5–8–7–6–5 patterns beginning in the *zona di passaggio* that move him immediately into *voce piena in testa*, or it may even be advisable for him to begin at A♮₄, on a descending 8–5–3–1 pattern, and then repeat the pattern a semitone or two higher.

EXERCISE 7.3

This pattern may be extended from the key of G to the key of B (with F♯₄ as the top note). Agile articulation is essential, with a good, clean release after the fermata. This series can also be profitably prefaced with the nasals [m], [n], and [ɲ]. The aim is for vital, but easy, production.

Another brief nonsustaining exercise that assists in achieving easier entry into upper-middle voice (and eventually into the region just above the *zona di passaggio*) consists of a brief repeated pattern at rapid tempo. The sixteenth notes should be sung as fast accented embellishments. Use alternating vowels at will (Exercise 7.4).

EXERCISE 7.4

After these agility exercises seem comfortable, vocalises of a more sustained nature can be introduced. Particularly recommended are short patterns that begin below the *primo passaggio* and progress into upper middle voice (see Exercises 7.5 and 7.6). Alternate front and back vowels.

EXERCISE 7.5

EXERCISE 7.6

Exercise 7.7 begins just below the *primo passaggio* and moves directly to the *secondo passaggio* area. (Choice of key should be slightly lower for a heavier voice, slightly higher for a lighter instrument.) Gradually this exercise, as well as the general *passaggio* vocalises, should be practiced in neighboring higher keys. Alternating front and back vowels should be used.

EXERCISE 7.7

Depending upon the already existing skills possessed by the emerging tenor, pitches above the *secondo passaggio* point may be approached either through intervallic leaps or consecutive pitch progressions. Some of the less-strenuous exercises earlier suggested for tenor *passaggio* work may be cautiously attempted. There is no magic in a particular pattern of pitches. Exercises that coordinate the three parts of the vocal mechanism (power source, vibrator, resonator) and liberate the singing instrument should be called upon.

The erstwhile baritone being reborn as a tenor needs to know that such an event is not sudden but gradual. The singer should first be absolutely certain that sound advice from a number of sources has been sought. Changing from baritone to tenor is a drastic career decision for an established singer. (It is, of course, much easier for the student baritone, but still requires time and patience.) The change of category ought not to be made when the predictable number of performing years ahead is limited. If reexamination of the basic premises of free vocal production (breath management, agility, resonation, vowel modification, the unified vocal scale, and vocal endurance) shows clearly that problems have resulted from the superimposition of baritone "color" on a tenor instrument, the change is appropriate.

There are some male voices that might well go in the direction of either a tenor or a baritone category. This is particularly true with the dramatic baritone who could be equally comfortable as a *robusto tenor* or even a

Heldentenor, or the light lyric baritone who could be comfortable with roles of a lower-lying tenor *tessitura.* (This is because of overlapping *passaggi* points between some baritone and tenor categories.) However, it may be that life will remain much easier if the monumental move into the heavier or high-lying tenor categories is not made. There are numerous instances of baritones who tried to make the transition without success, even thereby shortening their performance careers. Partially, the decision is an emotional and psychological as well as a physical one.

Very often an interesting pedagogical question is posed: if the young potential tenor is not comfortable singing any of the tenor literature, is it not advisable for him to sing for several years as a baritone? Would singing tenor immediately not be too strenuous and too discouraging?

Certainly, in such cases, the *tessitura* of high-lying tenor literature (particularly in a sizable potential tenor voice) should be avoided. But to classify the singer as a baritone and assign him baritone literature may not always be a wise move. Instead, the singer can be told that he is a potential tenor and that he should concentrate on medium-range literature. It is a mistake to have him attempt baritone aria literature while waiting to "discover" his upper range. Proper resonance balance is the immediate aim. If this is best achieved by singing some of the literature in medium keys, there is no harm. However, to try to make the young potential tenor *sound* like a baritone for several years and then to tell him he is a tenor is questionable pedagogical practice. Most professional singers once classified as baritones who later moved into tenor categories were originally misclassified and were encouraged to falsify the native timbre of their instruments. It is for this reason that proper vocal classification of a male voice is essential near the beginning of the technical journey.

One final word on this topic of the baritone/tenor dilemma may be appropriate. A certain number of young male voices are in flux because of mutation related to physical development. These singers have pleasant voices that seem limited on both ends of the vocal scale, yet they are musical and want to sing. Identifying the *passaggi* will be helpful, but the teacher should remember that every few passing months will bring about substantial developmental changes. Freeing the voice as an instrument will eventually reveal its classification. Classifying a young singer in his early months or even first year of study is not necessary. It is better pedagogy with such males to adopt a policy of wait and see.

THE PSYCHOLOGY OF SINGING TENOR

Performance anxieties beset every public performer at some point in a career. The more intense the performance responsibility, the higher will be the degree of anxiety. However, much performance anxiety is unnecessary. It is not foolish to experience fear if one is called upon to perform tasks that go beyond one's capabilities. To expect success during public singing of what has never gone well in the practice room or the voice studio is sheer folly. True, sometimes the flow of adrenalin during performance makes certain passages easier, but physical and emotional excitation is no substitute for technical skill.

Equally foolish is permitting oneself to be prey to performance anxiety about what always has gone well in practice sessions. The whole purpose of establishing vocal technique is to secure the acoustic and physical coordination that produces beautiful singing. One drills those coordinations and then calls upon them with assurance during performance, unless an uncontrollable condition, such as illness, intervenes. If a singer is unwell but must go ahead with a performance, he has every right to experience anxiety. Even then, a secure technique will pull him through.

Tenors are sometimes accused of being nervous performers. The point has already been made that much of what is demanded of the tenor goes beyond the requirements for other singers of elite vocal literature. There is no need to mention it again here, except to note that the tenor probably has considerable reason at times to be anxious. A conductor who takes one tempo at the dress rehearsal and another at performances (which is not an uncommon occurrence at all levels of competence) may cause more difficulties for the tenor than for other principals. For example, in the *Rigoletto* quartet, the Duke's task is far greater than that of the other singers. It is true that other singers also have moments of unusual responsibility, but the tenor has them with greater frequency. A lagging tempo or an unreasonable orchestral dynamic level is often more unfavorable for him than for other singers because of the nature of vocal writing for the tenor. However, tenors who sing literature appropriate to their particular vocal *Fach*, who have fine technical and musical foundations, and who are healthy probably exhibit no higher levels of performance anxiety than do other well-prepared singers.

For no other *Fach* is "the high note" surrounded with such expectation as it is in tenor literature. Even the coloratura soprano does not depend as heavily upon the climactic high note. Low notes for basses do not have the same dramatic impact as high notes for tenors. Baritones, whose registration events and ranges are often only a full tone below some of their tenor colleagues, are almost never required to maintain the high *tessitura* frequently demanded of tenors. (There are notable exceptions such as the *I Pagliacci* prologue or the baritone's vocal exploits in *Carmina Burana*.) The tenor repeatedly exhibits the ultimate pitches of his vocal range at the most exposed and dramatic and musical moments. Given the life he must lead on stage, the tenor may need to be the most technically secure and emotionally stable singer in the cast.

In the introductory remarks of this book it was noted that singing tenor requires courage; that sentiment may be a good one on which to close. Tenorial courage comes, in part, from being well prepared and from possessing a dependable technique. Courage is built on inner security as well. The more quietude and stability the singer has in his private life, the greater will be his professional calm. The wise tenor, planning a professional career, will search for an ordered life, a disciplined daily routine, secure musicianship, solid technique, good health habits, and supportive people around him. He will avoid emotional highs, temperamental eccentricities, performance superstitions, and harmful outside agents.

The purpose of artistic singing is to communicate beautiful sound to a listening public by means of expressive timbre, musical intelligence, and dramatic understanding. The responsible acceptance of those tasks, although they may be more demanding for the tenor than for any other vocal type, makes singing tenor highly rewarding.

International Phonetic Alphabet (IPA) Symbols

IPA SYMBOLS FOR VOWEL SOUNDS

IPA Symbol	English	German	Italian	French
		Vowels		
[i]	keen	Liebe	prima	lis
[ɪ]	thin	ich		
[e]	chaos	Leben	pena	été, crier
[ɛ]	bet	Bett, Gäste,	tempo	êtes, père neige
[æ]	bat			
[a]	task (American)			parle
[ɑ]	father	Stadt	camera	ras, âge
[ɒ]	hot (British)			
[ɔ]	soft, all	Sonne	morto	somme, joli, votre
[o]	note	Sohn	non	beaux, pauvre, gros
[ʊ]	nook	Mutter		
[u]	gnu, fool	Mut	uso	ou
[ʌ]	up			
[ə]	(schwa) ahead	getan		demain
[y] (approximates [i] plus [u])		müde		une,
[ʏ] (approximates [ɪ] plus [ʊ])		Glück		
[ø] (approximates [e] plus [o])		schön		peu,
[œ] (approximates [ɛ] plus [ɔ])		Köpfe		heure,

Vowel Sounds Peculiar to the French Language

[ɑ̃]				temps
[ɛ̃]				faim, vin,
[õ]				nom, long
[œ̃]				parfum, jeun

IPA SYMBOLS FOR SEMI-VOWELS (GLIDES) AND DIPHTHONGS

IPA Symbol	English	German		Italian		French
[j]	yes	ja		piú, pieno		lion, pied
[w]	wish			uomo, guida		moins
[aɪ]	nice	[ae]	Mai, Ei	[ai]	mai	
[aʊ]	house	[ao]	Haus	[au]	aura	
[eɪ]	way			[ei]	dovei	
[ɔɪ]	boy	[ɔø]	Häuser, Kreuz	[ɔi]	vuoi	
[oʊ]	so					

IPA SYMBOLS FOR CONSONANT SOUNDS

Pairs of consonants, one voiced and the other unvoiced, are executed with similar tongue and lip positions.

IPA Symbol	Voiceless	Classification by Formation	IPA Symbol	Voiced
[p]	pope	bilabial	[b]	bob
[t]	tote	lingua-alveolar	[d]	dead
[k]	coke	velar	[g]	glug
[f]	fife	labiodental	[v]	valve
[θ]	think	linguadental	[ð]	the
[s]	cease	dental	[z]	zones
[ʃ]	Sh!	lingua-alveolar	[ʒ]	vision
[ç]	ich (German)	palatal		
[x]	ach (German)	velar	[ ]	Paris (French)
[h]	ha-ha! (aspirate)	glottal	[ʔ]	uh-oh! (stroked glottal)
[tʃ]	chase	lingua-alveolar	[dʒ]	judgment
[ts]	tsetse	linguadental	[dz]	adds

As just indicated, the pairs are as follows:

[p]–[b]
[t]–[d]
[k]–[g]
[f]–[v]
[θ]–[ð]
[s]–[z]
[ʃ]–[ʒ]
[ç]–   ([ç] *is generally believed to be without a voiced counterpart*)
[x]–[ ]
[h]–[ʔ]
[tʃ]–[dʒ]
[ts]–[dz]

NASAL CONSONANTS

IPA Symbol		Classification by Formation
[m]	ma	bilabial nasal
[n]	no	alveolar nasal
[ŋ]	song	velar nasal
[ɲ]	ogni (Italian), onion (English), agneau (French)	palatal nasal
[ɱ]	conforto (Italian)	nasal labiodental

OTHER VOICED CONSONANTS

IPA Symbol	
[ʎ]	foglia (Italian)
[l]	lull
[ ]	rare (retroflex r, sometimes referred to as midwestern r)
[r]	very (single tap r, as in British speech)
[r̃]*	carro (Italian); Grund (German) (alveolar trill)

* The symbol [r̃] is used in many phonetic sources to represent the alveolar rolled r because the IPA symbol for the trilled r [r] is used indiscriminately in many American sources.

Spectrographic Analysis of Some Famous Tenor Voices

What makes the operatic tenor voice sound exciting to the listener? Are there common timbre characteristics to be found among all premier tenor voices? If so, what are they? How can they be determined? Spectral analysis may provide some answers to those questions.

It was already seen in Chapter 4 that several pedagogical parameters can be identified for a singer through the use of spectrographic analysis. Application of those analysis techniques to mature, top-drawer tenor singing artists produces some fascinating revelations.

Always to be taken into account are differences in recording ambiance and period technology pertinent to any recorded performance. Microphone characteristics, sound filtering, and audio engineering maneuvers vary from decade to decade and from one recording studio to another. However, certain acoustic attributes of the sounds of singing emerge unaltered, regardless of recording circumstances.

Passages here chosen for acoustic analysis are from much-beloved arias, sung by much-beloved tenors. Selections are from passages during which the singer is either momentarily unaccompanied by orchestral sound, or only lightly accompanied. Three tools are useful in determining timbre characteristics: (1) the spectrographic display, (2) the average power spectrum, and (3) the power spectrum. Each will be considered in turn.

SPECTROGRAPHIC DISPLAY

The technique of spectrum analysis was previously detailed in Chapter 4. In each of the phonations here under consideration, a spectrographic display of the passage analyzed appears in the lower window of each figure (see Figure B.1). The horizontal axis represents time, the vertical axis frequency. Degrees of darkness indicate levels of acoustic strength. (See Chapter 4 for a complete explanation of how phenomena such as vibrato, vowel definition, and singer's formant can be observed in spectrographic displays of this kind.)

AVERAGE POWER SPECTRUM

In the upper left-hand window, the horizontal axis represents frequency, the vertical axis intensity. In this analysis, the power spectrum is averaged between cursors 1 and 3 (being the two dotted vertical lines most left and right) shown in the spectrographic display.

POWER SPECTRUM

The right-hand upper window displays the power spectrum at cursor 2 (the dashed central cursor on the spectrographic display). The horizontal axis represents frequency, the vertical axis intensity. The "spectral envelope" of this graph resembles the average power spectrum when both graphs (the upper windows) present an analysis of the same phenomenon—in this case, a constant sound that is sung without change in pitch or vowel definition.

Texts are indicated above the spectrographic analysis not by actual syllabification but as the singer idiosyncratically joins changing phonetics. For that reason, texts are represented in the original language sounds, not by IPA symbols.

The first segment to be analyzed is the final *"pensier!"* from "La donna è mobile," (*Rigoletto*). The pitches are $F_4^\sharp$ and B_4 on the syllables *"pen"* [e] and *"sier"* [jɛ] respectively. It consists of an orchestra-free passage except for the beginning and the conclusion of the sustained B_4, at which point the orchestral sound is manifested by grey harmonic "smudginess." The four subjects are Jussi Bjoerling (Figure B.1), Franco Corelli (Figure B.2), Placido Domingo (Figure B.3), and Luciano Pavarotti (Figure B.4).

Figure B.1 (Bjoerling) is admirable in the cleanness of its distribution of acoustic strength; i.e., there is almost no indication of undesirable nonharmonic energy between the harmonic multiples of the fundamental frequency. In addition, the bandwidth terminates at about 3200 Hz, with little acoustic energy located above. Bjoerling's remarkable ability in combining lyricism and energy to produce beautiful vocal sound is apparent.

Figure B.2 (Corelli) demonstrates unusual strength in the second partial (1500 Hz), shown by the highest peak in the average power spectrum. Also of interest is the high concentration of acoustic energy in the region of the singer's formant (2500-3500 Hz). The relationships of these energy peaks are probably responsible for the *spinto* nature of Corelli's distinctive timbre.

Figure B.3 (Domingo) indicates a somewhat narrow vibrato excursion and a high energy level concentrated in the 3rd, 4th, and 5th partials of the fundamental frequency, with almost no acoustic energy occurring beyond 3100 Hz. This accounts for the modification of acoustic components so characteristic of this artist's singing, not typically found in some of his contemporary tenor colleagues.

Figure B.4 (Pavarotti) indicates tremendous levels of acoustic energy throughout the spectral bandwidth, even beyond (above 3500 Hz) the "traditional" upper boundary of the singer's formant. Further, the manner in which he combines vibrato parameters of cps., frequency excursion, and intensity leads to the perception of a grandiose production. The aesthetic and acoustic *chiaroscuro* aspects of classic international vocalism (elements of depth and brilliance) are evident in this thrilling phonation.

The spectrographic displays of Figures B.1 through B.4 also show two diverse stylistic routes for approaching a high note. Figures B.2 and B.3 (Corelli and Domingo) illustrate a *glissando* approach to the high B. In those phonations there is a 0.4 second adjustment during which resonance balance is altered. This "scooping" occurs between the termination of the sibilant [s] and the initiation of the pitch B_4 on the vowel [ɛ]. Figures B.1 and B.4 (Bjoerling and Pavarotti) show a markedly different approach: there is no *glissando*. The pitch B_4 then starts immediately without need to readjust the vocal tract and without loss in either vibrancy or purity of vowel definition. The aesthetic results verify the acoustic efficiency.

Although the next segment under consideration (the final climactic *"vincerò!"* from "Nessun dorma," (*Turandot*), with sustained B_4 on the syllable *ce*, followed by the sustained A_4 on the syllable *rò*) displays in all four graphs the presence of orchestrally generated sound, it nevertheless provides an excellent sample of how the four tenor voices considered above treat one of the most exposed moments in operatic performance.

Figure B.5 (Bjoerling) displays the same neatness of resonance balancing indicated in his *Rigoletto* passage. Bjoerling's inserted characteristic quick embellishment on the *rò* can be clearly observed, and indicates a remarkable ability to retain constant vibrancy at any tempo or frequency.

Figure B.6 (Corelli) exhibits extensive acoustic energy in the regions of the singer's formant, combined with great vibrancy. Considerable strength is also apparent in his prominent second partial. The degrees of darkness at the bottom of the graph indicate that the orchestra was at high decibel levels (as was Corelli!).

The phonation of Figure B.7 (Domingo) displays a somewhat brief encounter with the sustained B_4 and reveals a considerably narrower vibrato phenomenon (beginning nearly straight) on the B_4. The glissando through which the B_4 is reached demonstrates reductions in both vibrancy and acoustic strength. In returning to the final note on A_4 (*rò*), the vibrato stabilizes and the resonance balance exhibits great beauty.

Pavarotti's phonation in Figure B.8 is an exemplar *par excellence* of the energy and beauty of his amazing vocalism, with its completeness in pitch accuracy, constant vibrancy and overall vitality. The spacing of upper partials, the avoidance of undesirable nonharmonic acoustic energy between them, the rate of vibrato and extent of its excursion, and the intensity of his

Continued on p. 152.

FIGURE B.1. Spectral analysis of the voice of Jussi Bjoerling in the final "pensier" from "La donna è mobile" (*Rigoletto*).

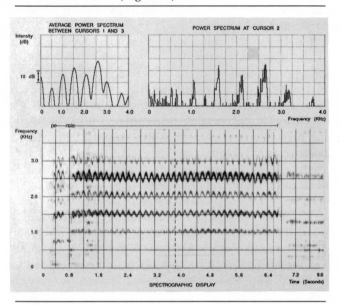

Rigoletto, RCA Records, ©1970. Conductor: Jonel Perlea. Orchestra: Rome Opera Orchestra and Chorus. Producer: Richard Mohr. Recording location: Rome Opera House, June 1956.

FIGURE B.2. Spectral analysis of the voice of Franco Corelli in the final "pensier" from "La donna è mobile" (*Rigoletto*).

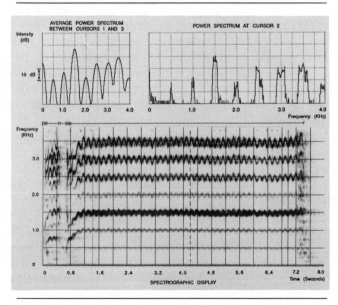

Prince of Tenors, Volume II, Legendary Recordings, (LR 198–2).

FIGURE B.3. Spectral analysis of the voice of Placido Domingo in the final "pensier" from "La donna è mobile" (*Rigoletto*).

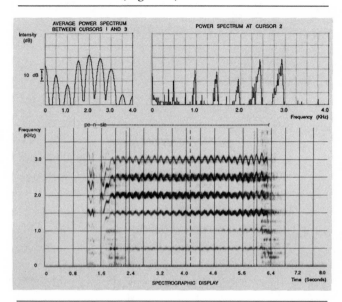

Bravissimo Domingo, RCA Red Seal, ©1985, 1982. Conductor: Erich Leinsdorf. Orchestra: London Symphony. Producer: Richard Mohr.

FIGURE B.4. Spectral analysis of the voice of Luciano Pavarotti in the final "pensier" from "La donna è mobile" (*Rigoletto*).

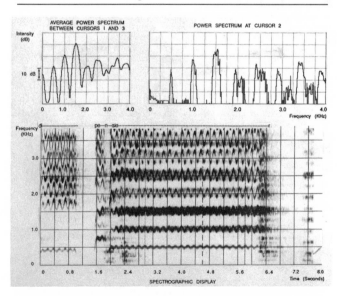

Rigoletto, London, ©1989. Conductor: Riccardo Chailly. Orchestra: Orchestra e Coro del Teatro Comunale di Bologna. Producer: Christopher Raeburn. Recording location: Teatro Comunale di Bologna.

FIGURE B.5. Spectral analysis of the voice of Jussi Bjoerling in the final "vincerò!" from "Nessun dorma" (*Turandot*).

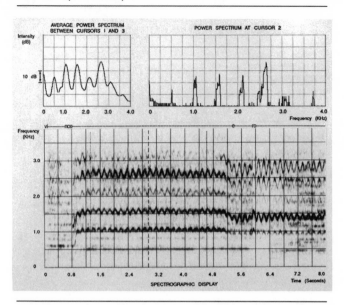

The Beloved Bjoerling, Volume 1, U.S.A. Capitol, 1961. Conductor: Nils Grevillius. Orchestra: Stockholm Concert Association Orchestra. Recording location: Europe, December 1936 to September 1948.

FIGURE B.6. Spectral analysis of the voice of Franco Corelli in the final "vincerò!" from "Nessun dorma" (*Turandot*).

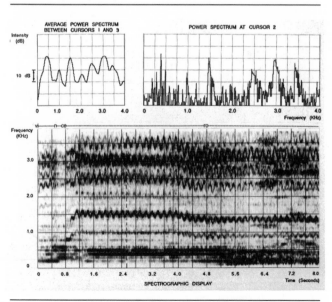

Turandot, EMI, ©1966. Conductor: Francesco Molinari-Prandelli. Orchestra: Opera and Chorus of the Opera House, Rome. Recording location: The Opera House, Rome.

FIGURE B.7. Spectral analysis of the voice of Placido Domingo in the final "vincerò!" from "Nessun dorma" (*Turandot*).

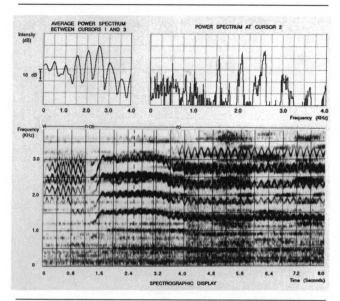

Turandot, Deutsche Grammophon, ©1982. Conductor: Herbert Von Karajan. Orchestra: Wiener Philharmoniker. Producer: Gunther Breest.

FIGURE B.8. Spectral analysis of the voice of Luciano Pavarotti in the final "vincerò!" from "Nessun dorma" (*Turandot*).

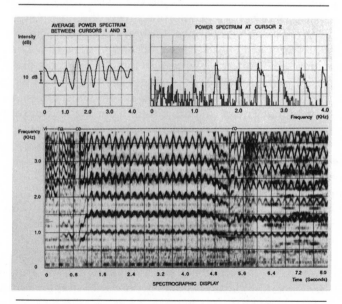

Carreras Domingo Pavarotti in Concert, London, ©1990. Conductor: Zubin Mehta. Recording producer: Christopher Raeburn. Recording location: Baths of Caracalla, Rome, July 1990.

FIGURE B.9.   Spectral analysis of the voice of Jussi Bjoerling in the "High-C passage" from "Che gelida manina" (*La Bohème*).

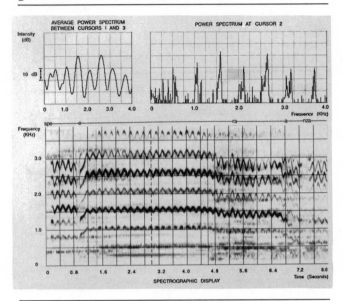

Great Artists at the Met, Met, 1936. Conductor: Nils Grevillius.
Orchestra: Stockholm Concert Association Orchestra.

sound as it soars above an extremely loud orchestral web, make this phonation viscerally, emotively, and interpretatively thrilling. As part of his attention to the completeness of vocal timbre, Pavarotti inserts an [ɑ] syllable within the word *"vincerò,"* so that it becomes "vin-*a*-ce-rò." Although this practice may be open to some question musically, a close examination of its occurrence here shows that the singer thereby maintains constant vibrancy and continuance of the legato. This is a trademark of some *verismo* vocal styles. Note that Pavarotti adopts the "Bjoerling embellishment" in this segment at exactly the same moment as does Bjoerling, thus retaining constant vibrancy. Although their voices are of different nature, size, and basic timbre, the productions of both Bjoerling and Pavarotti are characterized by great freedom, as this group of phonations attests.

Certainly one of the most celebrated of all moments in the operatic tenor literature is the "High-C passage" sung by Rodolfo in "Che gelida manina" (*La Bohème*). (The original version did not demand the C_5 expected today of a tenor. Under certain performance circumstances the aria is transposed so that B_4 replaces C_5 as the "high note." The C_5 phonations are chosen from recordings by Bjoerling, Domingo, and Pavarotti.)

Figure B.9 (Bjoerling) again exhibits great clarity in the phonation, by avoiding noise elements between harmonic partials, and by retaining constant vibrancy (momentarily interrupted by the insertion of an [h] in the

FIGURE B.10. Spectral analysis of the voice of Placido Domingo in the "High-C passage" from "Che gelida manina" (*La Bohème*).

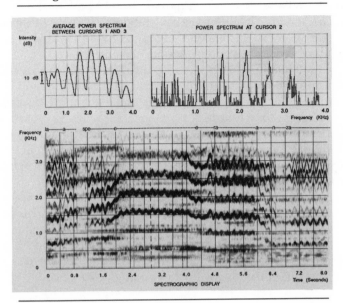

La Bohème, RCA Red Seal, ©1974. Conductor: Georg Solti. Orchestra: London Philharmonic Orchestra. Producer: Richard Mohr. Recording location: Walthamstow Town Hall, London.

FIGURE B.11. Spectral analysis of the voice of Luciano Pavarotti in the "High-C passage" from "Che gelida manina" (*La Bohème*).

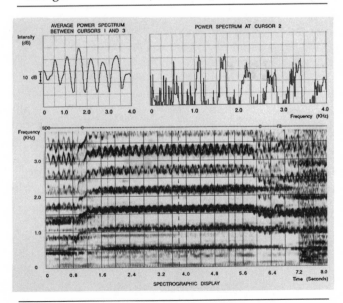

La Bohème, London, ©1973. Conductor: Herbert Von Karajan. Orchestra: The Berlin Philharmonic Orchestra.

middle of the syllable *"spe"* when moving from $A_4^\natural$ to C_5). En route to the $E_4^\flat$, the characteristic "Bjoerling embellishment" ($B_4^\natural$–C_5) is visible. An excellent model of vocal efficiency in singing is here provided, as is consistently the case with this wonderful tenor technician.

Figure B.10 (Domingo) displays a phonation in which this artist's normally pleasing vibrato rate narrows considerably at C_5, approaching a straight timbre. The *glissandi* approaching and leaving the C_5 also suggest degrees of straight-tone timbre.

Figure B.11. (Pavarotti) is remarkable in its duration of the C_5 as well as the extent of vibrancy and intensity. It should be noted that despite the differences in instrument and timbre, Bjoerling and Pavarotti approach the C_5 and return from it in similar fashion.

Extensive observations regarding these 11 phonations could be made. Without attempting detailed comparative study (thereby causing *primo uomo* wars among partisan admirers), suffice it to say that although spectral analysis reveals nothing the musical ear cannot hear when listening to great performers, it can graphically verify what the ear tells us, and testify to similar and dissimilar characteristics among great voices.

Glossary of Terms

Abduction: opening of the glottis.

Adduction: closure of the glottis.

Aggiustamento: vowel modification in singing; a method for achieving an even scale throughout the registers of the singing voice, associated with the historic Italian school.

Alveolus (pl. alveoli): small air cavity in the lung.

Aponeurosis: thick tissue that connects muscle to bone.

Appoggio: a technique, associated with the historic Italian school, for establishing dynamic balance between the inspiratory, phonatory, and resonatory systems in singing.

Arie antiche: vocal operatic literature from the early and (sometimes) late Baroque periods.

Arrotondamento: a rounding of vowels so as to diminish shrill or open singing in the course of the mounting scale, as practiced in the historic Italian school.

Bel canto: "beautiful singing," a term now frequently applied to the "classical" European solo vocal literature and singing style found prior to the middle of the nineteenth century; often narrowly restricted to the vocal writing (and performance practices) of Bellini, Donizetti, Rossini, and their contemporaries; used by extension to apply to styles of singing that stress vocal finesse over vocal power.

Breath cycle: process of inspiration and expiration.

Buccal cavity: cavity of the mouth; oral cavity.

"Call" of the voice: unmodified timbre in calling or yelling, detrimental to the singing voice in a *tessitura* above speech range.

Cantilena: a sustained melody in "singing" style.

Cavatina-cabaletta: aria, or scena form, of the *bel canto* period, consisting of a flowing graceful melody, followed by a florid and dramatic contrasting section; sometimes a recitative is interpolated between the two sections.

"Chest" voice: (see *voce di petto*).

Chiaroscuro tone: the "light-dark" timbre that characterizes well-balanced resonance in the singing voice.

Copertura: the technique of singing with *voce chiusa* timbre as opposed to *voce aperta* timbre, especially in the mounting scale, by using gradual vowel modification and by avoiding heavy laryngeal adjustment.

Countertenor: a singer who makes use of *falsetto* throughout much of his performance range; frequently a natural baritone.

Cover: a term often used to describe excessive laryngeal activity and exaggerated vowel migration that produce dark vocal timbre at *passaggi* pivotal points in the mounting scale. An exact definition of "cover" is not possible, because its meaning varies from one technique to another. (*Copertura* induces a gradual modification of vowels; *Deckung* requires more radical, sudden adjustments.)

Cricothyroids: paired muscles comprised of pars recta and pars obliqua, which attach to the front of the cricoid cartilage and alter the distance between the thyroid and cricoid cartilages, thereby stretching the vocal folds longitudinally.

Deckung: early and heavy "covering" as practiced in typically Germanic and Nordic techniques of singing.

Diaphragm: large muscle of the breath mechanism that divides the respiratory system from the digestive system.

Electromyography (EMG): a process for recording electrical energy generated by muscle activity.

Epigastric-umbilical area: upper part of the abdominal wall covering the area of the stomach and part of the viscera, extending from the navel to the sternum, erroneously called the diaphragm in some pedagogies.

Epiglottis: one of the three single cartilages of the larynx, located between the root of the tongue and the entrance to the larynx.

External frame structure of the neck: muscular system of the neck essential to establishing axial posture; serves as the external supportive musculature for the stabilized larynx.

External oblique: abdominal muscle whose fibers form layers of the lateral walls of the abdomen; fuses with the internal oblique at the linea alba; important in the *appoggio* system of breath management.

Fach: a German-language term meaning specific vocal category.

False vocal fold: (see ventricular fold).

Falsetto: the sound made by the male voice in imitation of the female voice.

Fioritura: ornament, cadenza, or florid passage.

Fistelstimme: (see *voce finta*).

Flageolet: an extension of the female upper voice, with a distinctive timbre.

Formant: a region of the spectrum displaying strong acoustic energy.

Fundamental frequency: the lowest in a series of partials, by which the listener perceives the pitch.

Gemischte Stimme: (see mixed voice).

Glottis: space between the vocal folds, which changes with abduction and adduction of the folds.

Harmonic partial: an overtone or upper partial; vibration frequency that is an exact multiple of the vibration rate of the fundamental frequency.

"Head" voice: descriptive term for sensations experienced during singing, particularly in upper range.

Heldentenor: a specialist in Wagnerian and other heavy roles, mostly of the Germanic repertory.

Hypogastrium: lowest of the three median areas into which the abdomen is divided by imaginary planes.

Hz (Hertz): unit of frequency (named for a German physicist), as in A–440.

Impostazione della voce (imposto): "placement" of the voice; a subjective term to describe the harmonic balance between the singer's formant and energy peaks in the lower part of the sung spectrum.

Intercostal muscles: short external and internal muscles between the ribs.

Internal oblique: abdominal muscles; they form the lateral walls of the abdomen and fuse with the external oblique to form the linea alba; important in the *appoggio* process of breath management.

Larynx (pl. larynges): the phonatory organ.

Lied (pl. Lieder): the German art song.

"Lifts": (see register breaks).

Linea alba: a median, tendinous line that separates the right and left sides of the abdominal musculature.

La lotta vocale (la lutte vocale, *Fr.*): the vocal contest (struggle); technique by which the inspiratory musculature offers opposition to the expiratory collapse of the breath mechanism; descriptive term for the *appoggio* technique.

Mélodie: the French art song.

Messa di voce: sustaining a note beginning at piano dynamic level, crescendoing to forte, then decrescendoing back to piano.

Mezzavoce: "half" voice; a vocal sound at piano level.

Middle voice: frequently used to designate the *zona di passaggio*; by extension, to include the lower-middle and upper-middle ranges of the voice, straddling "chest" and "head" registers.

Mixed voice: The region of the singing voice in which sensations of "chest" and "head" are simultaneously experienced; the *zona di passaggio*.

Mucosa: mucous membrane.

Occipital bone: bone in lower back portion of the skull.

Onset: (*l'attacco del suono; l'attacco;* attack): onset of voicing; the initial sound in singing.

Operetta tenor: a lyric tenor with extensive range who specializes in the operetta and musical comedy literatures.

Oscillation (wobble): a pedagogical term that refers to undesirably slow and wide pitch variations associated with vibrato.

Overtone: a harmonic partial higher than the fundamental.

Partial: (see harmonic partial).

Passaggio (pl. passaggi): vocal register pivotal point (as in *primo passaggio, secondo passaggio*).

Pelvis: the bony structure of the lower trunk.

Pharynx: part of the supraglottic resonator system, lying above the larynx and behind the mouth and nasal passages; comprising the laryngopharynx, the oropharynx, and the nasopharynx. (Popularly known as the "throat.")

Phonation: the production of vocal sound.

Place (Fr.): (see placement).

Placement: a subjective term that describes the harmonic balance that produces the singer's formant.

Primo passaggio: the first *passaggio* (see *passaggio*)

Pubic: (see hypogastrium).

Pyriform (Piriform) sinus: space between the laryngeal collar and the alae (wings) of the thyroid cartilage.

Rectus abdominis: a long, flat muscle located on either side of the linea alba and extending the length of the abdomen; it arises from the pubic crest and inserts into the cartilages of the fifth, sixth, and seventh ribs; its upper three-fourths is enclosed in the rectus sheath formed by the aponeuroses of the external and internal oblique muscles ventrally and the internal oblique and transversus abdominis dorsally; important to the postural coordination that produces the *appoggio* system.

Register: a series of consecutive voice tones of equal or similar timbre, which can be distinguished from an adjoining series of tones.

"Register breaks": a pedagogical term used by some teachers to describe register demarcations (see *passaggio*).

Release: termination of a sung phonation, coordinated with breath renewal; the new breath is the vocal release in skillful singing.

Resonator tube: in singing, the buccopharyngeal cavity, at times conjoined with the nasal cavity.

"Ring of the voice": resonance balance in the singing voice, the result of formant tuning and vowel tracking.

Secondo passaggio: the second *passaggio* (see *passaggio*).

Singer's formant: acoustic energy observable in spectra in the region of 2500–3300Hz (in the tenor voice).

Sitz: (see placement).

Sonagram: a kind of spectrograph (spectrum analysis graph).

Sostenuto: sustained singing.

Soubrette: a category of light soprano voice.

Spectral envelope: a visual representation graphing the component parts of a harmonic spectrum, with peaks and valleys indicating relative intensities.

Spectrograph: an electronic device that measures and records the harmonic components of phonation.

Spectrum: the sum of the acoustic factors of a sound, including the fundamental frequency and its component overtones.

Spieltenor: a category of tenor found in the German-language opera theater, similar in vocal character to the *tenore leggiero* but capable of a wider range of roles.

"Spreading": description of a tone that is blatant or "open"; the result of an unmodified vowel in ascending pitch.

Sternum: bone to which ribs are joined in the front of the thorax; popularly termed "the breast bone." Important to the positioning of the chest.

Strohbass: a male singing register that lies below pitches normally used in speech.

Subglottic: below the glottis.

"Support": voluntary respiratory control in singing; respiratory technique aimed at prolonging the inspiratory muscular gesture throughout much of the phonic event; the retardation of expiration through acquired control exercised over muscle groups involved in inspiration and expiration. (An inexact pedagogical term with a variety of meanings, some in opposition to each other.)

Supraglottic: above the glottis.

Tendon: a band of dense, fibrous connective tissue that provides attachment of muscle to bone.

Tenore buffo: a light tenor who specializes in comic opera roles.

Tenore di grazia: (see *tenore leggiero*).

Tenore drammatico: (see *tenore robusto*).

Tenore leggiero (tenore di grazia): a high-voiced male singer with an instrument of sufficient size and quality to be professionally viable; his repertoire includes florid vocal writing that requires agility and grace.

Tenore lirico: a lyric tenor who can sing much of the standard opera literature. He must have beautiful vocal timbre and be able readily to sustain a high *tessitura*.

Tenore lirico spinto: a large lyric instrument capable of performing repertoire such as the heavy Verdi roles.

Tenore robusto: the heaviest non-Wagnerian tenor voice, exhibiting exceptional power and stamina.

Tenorino: a high male voice of small size.

Tessitura: that part of the musical compass in which most of the pitches of a melody lie.

Thorax: the chest; upper part of the trunk.

Thyroarytenoids: two muscles rising below the thyroidal notch and inserting into each of the arytenoids.

Transverse abdominis: deep abdominal muscle, which with other abdominal muscles assists breath management.

Tremolo: a pedagogical term that refers to a vibrato rate too fast and too narrow (as distinct from wobble or oscillation).

Urkraft der Stimme: the primitive strength of the voice; part of a concept of breath damming originally advocated by Georg Armin; a popular approach to breath management among many Heldentenors, and among some Germanic teachers.

Velopharyngeal: pertaining to the region of the velum and the pharynx.

Velum: the muscular portion of the soft palate.

Ventricles of Morgagni (sinuses of the larynx): adjustable spaces lying between the true and false vocal folds.

Ventricular fold: false vocal fold, lying above the true vocal fold.

Vestibule of the larynx: the part of the laryngeal cavity above the false vocal folds.

Vibrato: a phenomenon of the singing voice; a pitch variant induced by the laryngeal muscles and related vocal tract areas in response to neurological impulses that occur when proper coordination exists between the breathing and phonatory mechanisms; a natural result in the singing voice of dynamic balancing of skillful airflow and free function in the mechanism of phonation.

Viscera: soft internal organs of the body, especially those of the trunk, such as the intestines.

Vocal fold: true vocal cord (also vocal band); paired muscles of the organ of phonation (larynx).

Vocal ligament: the edge of the vocal fold.

Vocal tract: the supraglottal resonator system.

Vocalis: the internal thyroarytenoid.

Voce aperta (open voice): "white," unskillful singing, lacking in proper resonance balance.

Voce bianca (voix blanche): white voice; open timbre as opposed to *voce chiusa.*

Voce chiusa (closed voice): balanced vocal timbre, avoiding *voce aperta.*

Voce di petto (chest voice; voix poitrine; Bruststimme): descriptive term for sensations experienced during singing in lower range.

Voce di testa: the head voice of the classic schools; a term based on resonance sensations during singing, not on actual resonator sources.

Voce finta: feigned voice; a timbre in the upper-middle range of the male voice that reduces the *voce piena* quality of the fully "supported" voice; at times confused with falsetto.

Voce media: (see middle voice).

Voce mista: (see mixed voice).

Voce piena in testa: full voice in "head" register (see head voice).

Voix mixte: (see mixed voice).

Vowel modification: gradual adjustment of vowels during the ascent of the scale so as to produce uniform timbre, resulting in an evenly registered voice.

"White voice": (see *voce bianca*).

Zona di passaggio: area of the voice where a number of tones can be sung by varying register emphases; middle voice.

Zygomatic arch: bony arch extending from the cheeks to the anterior sides of the skull.

Zygomatic bone: a bone of the side of the face, below the eyes.

Zygomatic muscle: a slender band of muscle on either side of the face, which rises from the zygomatic bone and inserts into the skin at the corners of the mouth.

Bibliography

Anatomischer Atlas (1979), ed. by Krmpotic Nemanic. Munich: Urban & Schwarzenberg.

Cunningham's Manual of Practical Anatomy (1977), ed. by G. J. Romanes. London: Oxford University Press.

Denes, Peter B., and Pinson, Elliot N. (1963). *The Speech Chain: The Physics and Biology of Spoken Language*. Philadelphia: Bell Laboratories (Dell Publishing).

Garcia, Manuel (1840). *Mémoire sur la voix humaine presenté à l'académie des sciences en 1840*. Paris: E. Surverger.

—— (1894). *Hints on Singing*, transl. by Beata Garcia. London: Ascherberg, Hopwood and Crew.

Gray's Anatomy (1980), ed. by Robert Warwick and Peter Williams. Edinburgh: Churchill Livingstone.

Jamieson, E. B. (1946). *Illustrations of Regional Anatomy*. London: E. & S. Livingstone.

Kantner, Claude E., and West, Robert (1960). *Phonetics*. New York: Harper Collins.

Klein, Hermann (1923). *An Essay on Bel Canto*. London: Oxford University Press.

Ladefoged, Peter (1974). *Elements of Acoustic Phonetics*. Chicago: University of Chicago Press.

Lamperti, Francesco (n.d.). *The Art of Singing*, transl. by J. C. Griffith. New York: G. Schirmer.

Minifie, Fred D.; Hixon, Thomas J.; and Williams, Frederick (1973). *Normal Aspects of Speech, Hearing and Language*. Englewood Cliffs, New Jersey: Prentice Hall.

Proctor, Donald F. (1980). "Breath, the Power Source for the Voice," *The NATS Bulletin*, Nov/Dec.

Schutte, H. K. and Miller, Richard (1984). "Resonance Balance in the Register Categories of the Singing Voice: A Spectral Analysis Study." *Folia Phoniatrica*. Basel: S. Karger.

—— (1985a). "Breath Management in Repeated Vocal Onset." *Folia Phoniatrica*. Basel: S. Karger.

—— (1985b). "Intraindividual Parameters of the Singer's Formant." *Folia Phoniatrica*. Basel: S. Karger.

Stevens, Kenneth H., and Hirano, Minoru (1981). *Vocal Fold Physiology*. Tokyo: Tokyo University Press.

Titze, Ingo (1987). "Nasality in Vowels." *The NATS Journal*, Mar/Apr.

—— (1981). "What Determines the Elastic Properties of the Vocal Folds and How Important Are they?" *The NATS Bulletin*, Sep/Oct.

Topographische Anatomie (1935), ed. by Wilhelm Lubosch. Munich: J. F. Lehmanns Verlag (Springer-Verlag).

van den Berg, Janwillem (1968). "Register Problems." *Sound Production in Man: Annals of the New York Academy of Sciences*, ed. by A. Bouhuys. New York: New York Academy of Sciences.

—— (1964). "Some Physical Aspects of Voice Production," *Research Potentials in*

Voice Physiology, ed. by David Brewer. Syracuse, NY: State University of New York.

Vennard, William (1967). *Singing: The Mechanism and the Technique*. New York: Carl Fischer.

Index

Numbers in italics refer to glossary terms.

A

Abdominal
  compression, 24
  distention, 24, 25, 26
  movement (inward), 17
  muscles, 15, 16, 18, 19, 20–23, 24,
    26, 27, 37, 88
  viscera, 16, 17, 20, 25
  wall, 15, 16, 17, 20, 24, 25, 26, 30,
    31, 32, 88, 90
Abduction, 7, 8, 27, 29, 31, *155*
Acoustic
  analysis, 42, 77, 79, 84, 146–54
  energy (strength), 41, 71, 72, 73,
    74, 75, 76, 81, 120, 146, 147
Adam's apple. *See* Laryngeal: promi-
    nence
Adduction, 7, 8, 29, 31, *155*
Aerodynamic/myoelastic factors, 15,
    24, 88
aggiustamento, 39, 41, 46, 48, 49, 56,
    57, 58, *155*. *See also* Vowel: modi-
    fication
Agility, 87–104, 136, 137
Aïda (Verdi), 12
Airflow, 3, 8, 15, 17, 19, 24, 27, 28,
    32, 48, 79, 80, 125, 128, 130,
    135
Alfredo (*La Traviata*), 11
Almaviva (*Il Barbiere di Siviglia*), 10,
    87, 96–97, 102–4
Almaviva/Figaro duet (*Il Barbiere di
    Siviglia*), 96–97, 102–4
Alveolus (alveoli), 17, 19, *155*
Am Meer (Schubert), 107–8
Anxiety. *See* Performance anxiety
Aponeurosis, 24, *155*
Appendicular body, 24, 25
Appoggio, 14, 16, 25, 26, 27, 28, 30,
    31, 32, 37, 43, 88, 124, *155*
Ariadne auf Naxos (Strauss), 12
arie antiche, 132, *155*

arrotondamento, 39, 58, *155*
Articulation, 88, 126
  aspirated, 87, 95
  impulses, 31, 90–91, 93
  legato, 95
Arturo (*Lucia di Lammermoor*), 10
Aryepiglottic folds, 38, 48
Arytenoid cartilage, 7, 8, 38, 39, 48
Atmospheric pressure, 19
Axial
  alignment (position), 24, 25, 26, 67,
    124, 125, 126
  body, 20, 24, 25

B

Bacchus (*Ariadne auf Naxos*), 12
Bach, Johann Sebastian, 9, 13
Back vowels, 42, 43, 53, 54, 57, 58,
    59, 74, 81, 83, 84, 123
"Bad vowel," 83
Ballo in maschera, Un (Verdi), 12
Barbiere di Siviglia, Il (Rossini), 10, 87,
    96–97, 102–4
Bardolfo (*Falstaff*), 11
Baritone, 11, 12, 13, 38, 105, 130,
    133–38, 139
Baroque and early music, 9, 95, 129,
    132
Bartered Bride, The (Smetana), 10
Bass, 105, 131, 134, 139
bel canto, 87, 93, 106, 131, *155*
Bellini, Vincenzo, 10, 87, 131, 132
Beppe (*I Pagliacci*), 10
Bizet, Georges, 58, 61–62
Bjoerling, Jussi, 146, 147, 148, 150,
    152, 154
Body alignment. *See* Axial: alignment
Bohème, La (Puccini), 11, 12, 48, 50,
    58, 60, 88, 89–90, 105, 152, 153
Boito, Arrigo, 109, 112
Boris Godunov (Mussorgsky), 10